Unexplained Oxford and Oxfordshire

by
Marilyn Yurdan

The
Book
Castle

First published October 2002
by
The Book Castle
12 Church Street
Dunstable
Bedfordshire LU5 4RU

ISBN 1 903747 21 X

Typeset and Designed by Priory Graphics
Flitwick, Bedfordshire
Printed by Print Solutions Partnership,
Wallington, Surrey

Front cover: Magpie Lane, Oxford
Back cover: The Birdcage, Thame

CONTENTS

THE AUTHOR

Marilyn Yurdan was born in Oxford and her family has lived in the county for generations. She went to grammar school in a building which occupies an ancient and haunted site, which awakened her interest in both the history of the area and in those aspects of life which defy rational explanation. Since 1984, she has been Assistant Custodian at the Sheldonian Theatre, Oxford, which offers plenty of scope for involvement in all the University's colourful customs and traditions.

Marilyn Yurdan is a graduate of Oriel College and has a Master's degree in English Local History. Her other publications are *A Guide to Family History, Tracing Your Ancestors, Oxfordshire and Oxford, Irish Family History and Oxford Town and Gown.* She is also a regular contributor to *The Oxford Times* 'Limited Edition' magazine. In addition to local and family history, her interests include photography (as seen in this book), gardening and her three elderly tortoises.

UNEXPLAINED OXFORD AND OXFORDSHIRE:

AN INTRODUCTION

Oxfordshire is one of the least explored of the southern counties, overshadowed as it is by its county town and university. Visitors may visit Woodstock because of Blenheim Palace, or Burford en route for the Cotswolds, or travel along the Thames Valley as far as Henley, but how many venture off the main roads in search of Marsh Baldon, Pudlicote or Piddington?

It is not an exceptional county in any way; everything in Oxfordshire is on a comfortable, human scale, and it is in this ordinariness that its appeal lies. The majority of its settlements are typical small English towns and villages, neither ruined, as yet, by development nor quaint. They are quirky, individualistic and full of personality. Most have something of interest to reward the visitor, whether it be attractive, gruesome, historic or tragic.

Situated near the heart of England, both geographically and historically, Oxfordshire can boast a temporary capital, vital route and communication centre, and the oldest university in the English-speaking world in its county town. Furthermore, three, if not four, kings were born within its boundaries: Alfred the Great at Wantage, Edward the Confessor at Islip, Richard the Lionheart, and almost certainly John, in Oxford.

For the purposes of this book, Oxfordshire may be conveniently divided up into six sections: the City and University of Oxford; the Greater Oxford area; West Oxfordshire lying to the west and north west of Oxford; Cherwell, the northern and central portion; South Oxfordshire, and the Vale of White Horse which it acquired from Berkshire on the county boundary changes of 1974.

These divisions offer examples of the differing aspects of the English countryside. To the west several small rivers make their leisurely way from the Cotswolds to the Thames, and, once again, the privacy of the smaller settlements is safeguarded by the A40, which conveys much of the traffic onwards into the West Country and Wales. This is a region of close communities and, apart from at Carterton, the dormitory village for the airforce base at Brize Norton, there has been little infiltration by newcomers until recently. West Oxfordshire has long memories and its distinctive

1

dialect shows close affinities with Thomas Hardy's Wessex to the south-west.

The northern part shows the proximity of the Midlands, with its iron-stone buildings and the flattened vowels of its residents. The main tourist route from London to Stratford upon Avon goes north from Oxford along the A34, leaving the villages thereabouts largely untouched and unexplored.

The southern part of historical Oxfordshire stretches from Oxford itself to the Thames Valley where it becomes classic Thames and Chilterns countryside with water meadows, with riverside moorings, and leafy lanes winding among chalk hills to tiny villages with beech woods and ancient churches. Near the river itself is true stockbroker country, evidence of the nearness of London.

Oxfordshire now includes the remote little communities in the Vale of White Horse, while Abingdon, the former county town of Berkshire, is now officially the English town which can prove longest continuous habitation. The vale is strewn with relics of our remote ancestors: burial mounds and barrows, camps, hill forts and the ancient White Horse himself, cut out of the chalk hillside. This area is real Wessex, both historically and according to Hardy, whose village names reflect the character and past of the real ones. Wantage, for example, becomes Alfredston in his novel *Jude the Obscure*.

The county town is probably the most haunted place in England, an ideal setting for assorted ghosts and spectres to flit around, as Jude evidently thought, for on his first night in 'Christminster' he immediately began to people the deserted streets with phantoms ancient and modern, dead and still living, of members of the University.

Throughout this book the terms 'ghost' or 'phantom' have been used for anything which was unexplained at the time of the incident, whether or not there was a sighting – in short those things to which the human mind is unable to give a satisfactory explanation according to the limits of its own experience.

The main source of material is the 'Hauntings' file of the Oxford and County Newspapers group, plus the results of articles published by the Oxford Star, and an interview on what was then BBC Radio Oxford. Although the majority of the entries are modern, authenticated accounts, some which have passed into local folklore have been included. These are found in old guides and travel books which frequently mention hauntings, sometimes as old wives' tales, sometimes facetiously, but usually in a matter-of-fact way. Several such accounts have been included because they are amusing or interesting in their own right and form part of the oral and written traditions of the county.

The ghost is timeless in that it may manifest itself as an Ancient Briton, a Roman soldier, a medieval lady, or an Edwardian child. It need not take on human form; animal ghosts exist, as do apparitions of inanimate objects, like various modes of transport. Neither need the hauntings be visible, some consisting of footsteps, perfumes, moans or knocks.

Specimens of most types of British haunting are recorded in Oxfordshire, although there is no distinctly regional type of ghost, no Black Shuck, no Little People, no wailing, disembodied presences, no elementals and no real vampires.

The county has so many examples of spectral nuns and monks, and their relatives, the grey, white, and brown ladies, that one tends to become somewhat blasé about them. This type of sighting has therefore been included only when it took place in an interesting location, or where there seems to be historical justification for a ghost to appear.

Another type of haunting found in every corner of Oxfordshire involves the use of water, or some stronger liquid, in the laying of a troublesome spirit. This idea seems to be particularly common in West and central Oxfordshire, and has a strong connection with the Islamic idea of *djinn*, spirits who live near water and must be imprisoned in some sort of vessel. These must be relations of Aladdin's genie of the lamp.

In some cases, a particular haunting is assigned to a named individual, usually a former resident of a building, such as a public house, a farm or a school. In these cases the ghost is usually given a name and a story found, or invented, to explain its presence. Favourite heroes and heroines are the suicidal lover, the wronged servant girl, the repentant wrongdoer, and the victim of a murder. The villain is the seducer, oppressor or murderer himself, condemned to walk this earth until he expiates his crime.

This Introduction serves merely as an aperitif to some of the unexplained delights which Oxfordshire has to offer. Somebody's favourite haunting is certain to have been left out, some omissions being deliberate, chiefly due to lack of convincing evidence, others because one has to decide where to draw the line before the book becomes repetitive. It has been very difficult to choose between all the monks and nuns, shapes and figures, sounds and smells, coaches and carriages, footsteps and knocks.

Banbury
Souldern
Deddington
Over Norton
Chipping Norton
Enstone
Steeple Aston
Fringford
Kingham
Spelsbury
Bicester
Charlbury
Launton
Kirtlington
Weston
Ascott
Stonesfield
Woodstock
Piddington
Burford
North Leigh
Yarnton
Witney
Charlton
Eynsham
Kidlington
Beckley
Oxford
Wheatley
Stanton
Harcourt
Thame
Bampton
Rycote
Cowley
Marsh Baldon
Abingdon
Clifton Hampden
Faringdon
Chamey
Bassett
Long Wittenham
Sutton
Courtenay
Wallingford
Grove
Wantage
Ginge
W. Hendred
Henley on
Thames

4

CHAPTER ONE:
OXFORD CITY AND UNIVERSITY

*Tourist Information Centre, 15-16 Broad Street, Oxford OX1 2DA.
Tel: 01865 726871*

Many of Oxford's ghosts have not been sighted for years and yet receive regular coverage in guidebooks and local periodicals, especially in the period before Hallowe'en or at Christmas. No one can prove or disprove their existence and they all go into the melting pot which, over the centuries, has produced the rich and varied folklore of Oxford.

It is doubtful, for example, if anyone today would claim to have seen the well known ghost of Colonel Windebanke, said to haunt **Deadman's Walk** which runs along south of the city wall between Rose Lane and the Christ Church Meadows exit into Merton Street. The Colonel, who was newly married, was shot in the vicinity for cowardice, by Prince Rupert, because, it was alleged, he had surrendered the Oxford garrison to Parliament. However, Deadman's Walk does not take its name from this execution, but from the fact that Jewish funeral parties took this route in the early Middle Ages going from the Jewish quarter in St Aldate's to its burial ground where the Botanic Garden is now.

The Roundhead soldier, reported in the Oxford Mail, of 11th October 1966 to have been sighted in **Charles Street**, may or may not have had a connexion with Colonel Windebank, but the soldier like the street seems to have fallen victim to the Westgate development.

In a room above **Ducker's**, the well-known boot and shoemakers in Turl Street, an elderly basket work armchair appears. It is very ordinary, worn and looks comfortable, although it only materialises for a few seconds, then gradually fades away, like the Cheshire Cat, into nothing. This chair is

Deadman's Walk

mentioned by Jan Morris (in *Oxford*, Oxford, 1978), but again, no modern or authenticated sightings have been reported. Similarly, according to the local student paper, Isis, 5th June 1968, the cellar of **Lincoln College** in Turl Street, is supposed to be haunted by the ghosts of 20 men who suffocated there.

A room on the first floor of Staircase 12 in St Mary's Quad at **Oriel College**, Oriel Square, abuts the wall of the Junior Common Room which was once the chapel of St Mary College, later absorbed by Oriel. Stephen Usherwood, who came up to Oriel in 1926, writes in the Oriel College Record, 1995, how his scout had informed him that in the night he would hear 'the heart of the bishop beating'. The bishop in question was Cardinal William Allen, Principal of St Mary Hall from 1556. There is no record, unfortunately of the heart's actually having been heard.

Luckily, the following unexplained happenings in Oxford do have impeccable references.

The College of All Souls of the Faithful Departed, in High Street, was founded in 1428 by King Henry VI as a memorial to his father Henry V, and all those who fell in the Hundred Years War. All Souls is unique in that all its members are Fellows, there being no undergraduate or graduate students. Oliver Cromwell used to lodge at the College during his Chancellorship of the University between 1651 and 1657.

All Souls' best-known idiosyncrasy is the Mallard Hunting Ceremony which takes place every hundred years, on 14th January in the first year of the new century. The Warden, as Head of the College, leads a procession carrying lighted torches and allegedly searching for the legendary mallard which is reported to have flown up out of a drain when the foundations of the College were being laid. As they march round they sing the Mallard Song, a ditty which is also performed at All Souls gaudies, or gatherings, in the intervening years. It is essential that the song is never heard by an outsider. The Lord Mallard is carried round in a sedan chair, in procession, with a dead duck suspended on a pole as an accessory. They process three times round the quadrangle, and then go up onto the roof, still in search of the elusive game bird.

After all this splendid eccentricity, it is disappointing to relate that the All Souls ghost is nothing more original than a white-robed man who emerges from a spot near the door to the chapel, and makes his way to the library where he disappears.

Oriel College, St. Mary's Quad

The Castle Bridge area of Oxford has long had a reputation for being haunted. In 1071, Robert D'Oilly, governor of Oxford, built a large, well-defended castle to the west of the Saxon city, in order to subdue the native population. Its main entrance was in Castle Street, behind the County Hall. During the winter of 1142, Queen Mathilda was besieged in the castle by her rival and cousin, Stephen. Dressed entirely in white, she managed to escape across the snowy fields and along the frozen Thames, to the safety of Wallingford castle. Today, visitors accompanied by an official guide may descend a stone staircase into Oxford Castle Mound, which, together with the tower of the chapel of St George-in-the-Castle, is the only survivor of this once mighty structure.

Most Oxonians will have heard that there is 'something' which haunts this area, although few will be able to give any details. This appears to be a remnant of the story of the three Maidens Kendall (Oxford Times, 24th December 1976) who were great benefactors of the nearby church and parish of St Thomas, in the seventeenth and eighteenth centuries. The eldest of these, Anne, instigated several parish charities according to the terms of her will when she died in 1714. All three Maidens would appear regularly on Quarter Days, dealing out largesse to the poor of the district, and were recognisable, as in life, by their dresses of grey silk. Some unsociably minded person attempted to arrange an exorcism, but to no avail, despite the efforts of several clergymen. The Kendall sisters persisted in continuing their good work, and it was not until thirteen bishops, no less, intervened, that they gave way.

Many people, however, remained unconvinced that the bishops had in fact succeeded, and rumours continued to circulate, including one featuring a certain Rewley House near what is now Worcester Street and Gloucester Green. This was said to be haunted by a lady wearing a grey silk dress, who would watch children at play. The house, which had latticed windows and was very ancient, was the Kendall family home, but has long since been demolished. Despite this fact, the lady continued to scare local children well into the twentieth century, by her old fashioned dress and the fact that she would disappear whenever they tried to speak to her.

Exeter College, in Turl Street, was founded by Walter de Stapledon, Bishop of Exeter, in 1314. Originally called Stapledon Hall, it changed its name to Exeter Hall in the mid-fourteenth century, and finally took its

Castle Tower

present name in the fifteenth. It is known as the West Countryman's College
due to its Founder being a Devon man.

The chapel houses the well known Magi tapestry designed by
Burne-Jones and executed by William Morris, two leading members of the
Pre-Raphaelite brotherhood. The chapel was rebuilt in the 1850's.

All that remains of the medieval college is the gate tower (1432, cleaned and restored 1968, known as Palmer's Tower, it is where a headless man was once in the habit of throwing himself from the summit in a reinactment of some long forgotten tragedy.

A peculiar form of haunting took place on No 6 Staircase, the person involved being Dr Thomas Wood, then an undergraduate and later a famous composer. The story was featured in the Oxford Mail of 2nd November 1966, exactly half a century after the event took place.

Wood had rooms at the top of the staircase, five flights up, and, on October 31st 1916, was on the point of leaving to attend a coffee party in a friend's rooms. He had already turned out the light prior to closing the door when he stopped suddenly in his tracks, frozen by what he saw in the doorway.

"A man was standing right up against me with the narrow band of light under Sharp's door shining through his body, and he had no head. Words won't come fast enough, buff coat; yellow slashings; black gown; one hand up as though he were going to knock; the bright pinpoint of Sharp's keyhole where his heart should be, and where his face should be. . . nothing. He stood still while I could have counted one, two, three, four, and my hair bristled. Then he went - puff - out like a candle."

Needless to say, an immediate search was carried out, but nothing untoward was found. Wood came in for a good deal of teasing for having dreamed up such an apparition without benefit of alcohol, even though it had happened at Hallowe'en.

The next day, however, he heard a strange and very interesting story related to him by his tutor. The previous morning, the very one when Wood had met the apparition, work had started on clearing out junk and unwanted items from beneath No 6 Staircase. By the evening the workmen had shifted most of the rubbish and had discovered a statue. This seemed to be of a man in seventeenth-century costume and was quite battered, but still of considerable historical interest. At his tutor's invitation, Wood went down to the basement to see the statue, and found it to be a small figure of a man kneeling at prayer.

"He was wearing his gown and a tunic that had slashed sleeves edged with lace around the wrists. Faint traces of colour were left: brown. He had no head. My hair bristled for the second time. I had seen the original of this battered piece of marble. He came to knock at my door last night."

On further investigation, Wood discovered that his visitor was identical to a monument erected to John Crocker, a gentleman-commoner from Devon, who had been a member of the College and had died on 29th April 1629. It seems that the statue had been hidden away in the basement under No 6 Staircase since the seventeenth-century chapel had been destroyed in the 1850's, but why John Crocker had waited until 1916 to manifest himself remains a mystery. Presumably, the rediscovery of his statue had given him the idea. Did he appear at the time of the chapel's demolition, perhaps? And why did he choose to go up five flights of stairs to visit Wood in particular? Whatever the answer, he was locked away behind the massive doors of the present chapel, in case he decided to frighten other Hallowe'en revellers in the years to come.

Jesus College, in Turl Street, was founded in 1571 by Dr Hugh Price, under the patronage of Queen Elizabeth I. It is called the Welshman's College, because of the nationality of its founder and the fact that most of its benefactors were from Wales; today, it continues its links with the Principality.

The oldest part of the college fabric is the sixteenth-century Turl Street frontage, through which one reaches Front Quad with the Chapel on its north side, and Hall on the west, both seventeenth-century buildings.

A 'living ghost' story was told by Mr P-J, who had rooms right at the top of No 1 Staircase in Front Quad. The year was 1910, and P-J was entertaining a friend, also a college member. Around midnight, during a break in the conversation, the two students made their way over to the window and stood looking down on the Quad which was bathed in moonlight. There they caught sight of their tutor, a Mr J, who was strolling up and down between Hall and Chapel, apparently enjoying the night air before going to bed. After watching him for a few minutes, P-J and his friend decided to pop downstairs and follow Mr J, and walk behind him as he patrolled the Quad. They scuttled down the staircase, hid themselves in a dark porch and, as the tutor executed a smart about-turn, slipped out of the darkness and marched along behind him. Emboldened, they then proceeded to whistle Mr J's favourite hymn tune, "All Through the Night", as befits a Welshman. To their surprise and disappointment, he took not the slightest bit of notice, but continued to stroll as if he were quite unaware of their presence. After they had followed him for a minute or two and had begun to narrow the distance between them, the tutor reached the end of

the pavement. Just as he would have been forced to turn round and meet them head on, he kept on walking - straight through the six-foot thick wall of the Hall!

The friends stopped dead, and stared unbelievingly. Then they hurried over to the place where Mr J had vanished into the masonry. Frantically, they hunted about in the thick, knotted ivy covering the walls, but of course they found nothing at all.

In 1968, some 58 years after the incident, Mr P-J, then aged 81, remembered every detail clearly, and described it in Isis, 5th June 1968.

"It was frightening and inexplicable. We were certain when we first saw the figure from my upstairs room that it was Mr J. We would not have rushed down to play this prank on him had we not been certain that it was our tutor, and even when we saw him in full view from the porch it never entered our heads that it was not Mr J taking a midnight walk. We could see his white tie which was popular with non-conformist Welsh clergymen of the time, and every feature of his face was visible. When we looked in the ivy when it had disappeared, we were both scared stiff, and beat a retreat back up to my room. To this day no rational explanation has ever occurred to me."

The next day, the undergraduates set about establishing the whereabouts of Mr J on the night in question, and found out that he had been staying with relatives at nearby Wolvercote.

Magdalen College, right at the eastern end of the High Street, was founded in 1458 by the then Bishop of Winchester, William of Wayneflete, on the site of the medieval Hospital of St John the Baptist. Its Bell Tower (1492-1509) is a local landmark, and along with Christ Church's Tom Tower is a symbol of Oxford worldwide. Here, on May Morning, the College choir sings its hymn to welcome in the Spring. They sing from only three sides of the tower, because, as rumour has it, a chorister once fell to his death from the fourth side. After the singing is over, the bells of Oxford ring out and festivities are under way.

Through Cloister Quad lies the New Building, new, that is, in 1733, its colonnade reached across an extensive lawn. Adjoining it is one of the college's main attractions, the Grove, which has been a deer park since the beginning of the eighteenth century.

In the Trinity, or Summer, Term, 1968, CR, a Second Year student, arose

Magdalen College and Bridge

early one Sunday morning in order to write an essay. About 5.45, 'before the deer were awake', as he told *Isis*, 5th June 1968, he left his room and walked along under the colonnade arches, noticing as he went that the grass was still covered in dew. CR was glancing in the direction of the Cloisters when he caught sight of a black shape heading in his direction. As it came closer, and he was able to get a better view, he could see that it was the silhouette of what seemed to be a headless figure dressed in some sort of robe.

"It was walking in a straight line towards staircase 3, the next one to mine. Its clothes did not move as it came across the lawn and it made no sound at all. There were no ordinary walking movements even when it mounted the three steps into the colonnade it appeared to glide rather than walk and still there was no ordinary swirling of the robe: it remained fixed. As it drew level with me in the colonnade I stared hard at the figure and where its head should have been I could only see the wooden door twenty yards further on at the end of the arches. Even on the stone pavement of the colonnade, there was no sound of movement or footsteps. As the figure approached the entrance to staircase 3 and came into a stronger light, it simply vanished from view. I never expected to see a ghost: I always thought that ghosts were white and made horrible noises. This one was black and silent and its limbs appeared not to move as it glided along. I have never thought up a rational explanation even though I've often tried; the apparition defied the rational faculties."

What CR did not know at the time that he had his sighting, was that a few weeks earlier a First Year historian, RS, was making his way across the same lawn between 11 p.m. and midnight, when he happened to look to his left. RS then caught sight of "a black silhouette keeping pace with me as I walked towards the colonnade. The figure kept pace exactly with me and I kept glancing to my left to look at it. There was no sound of footsteps. We went up the few steps under the arches together; it was about ten yards away. When I looked to my left after passing under the arch and into the colonnade, I expected to see it still keeping pace with me, but it had disappeared completely."

CR and RS had not spoken to each other about their experiences, and it was not until an investigation was carried out by Isis that they discovered that they had both seen an identical black figure which had disappeared at exactly the same spot in the colonnade at Magdalen.

On a dark night in November 1975, sixteen-year-old Jane Jones and her mother Julie were driving across **Magdalen Bridge** when they saw a strange figure in front of the car. It was a man in tweed, sitting very upright, on a rickety old black bike. The strangest thing about him, however, was that he was without a head. Jane turned to her mother to ask, "Did you see what I've just seen?" Her mother nodded. They decided not to mention the incident to anyone else.

Some years later, Jane came across an account of accidents which had taken place in Oxford, and suddenly found a reason for what they had seen on Magdalen Bridge, that November night. It seems that in the first half on the twentieth century, an undergraduate was involved in an accident on the bridge, and had his head taken off.

Another ghostly tale concerning the bridge tells of a man who was returning home when, in the mist, he saw a dark figure which appeared to fall over the bridge into the river below. He told the police, but they were not unduly worried, being quite used to similar reports of a 'black man' falling off the bridge. They had, in fact, dragged the river on previous occasions, but nothing had been found.

This could well be an enactment of the shooting of a chimney sweep who was involved in a riot over the election of 1750, and who fell into the river and drowned. As the marksman was not punished for his actions, the sweep seems to feel it necessary to reappear in an effort to remind passers by.

On the corner of Magpie Lane, which leads southwards off the High Street, is the former Barclays Old Bank, now the **Old Bank Hotel**. When the premises were used by the Bank, a well known haunting was that of Prudence, said to be a Puritan maid who had the misfortune to fall in love with a Cavalier. Whether this ill-fated love was thwarted, or simply unrequited, is not on record, but legend has it that Prudence killed herself because of it. She must have been buried in consecrated ground, for the burial registers of St Mary the Virgin opposite record her as Prudence Burcote, with no mention of suicide. The bank staff were matter-of-fact about Prudence's visits, most of which consisted of footsteps and rustlings, rather than actual sightings, although she has appeared on several occasions. Time will tell whether or not she will continue to patronise the premises now that they have been converted into a hotel.

Magpie Lane

Merton College, Merton Street, was founded in 1264 by Walter de Merton, and served as a pattern for later colleges, notably Peterhouse, Cambridge, which specifically mentions Merton's statutes. Merton's claim to be Oxford's oldest college, one which it disputes with Balliol and University Colleges, is by virtue of its being the first to build its own premises, rather than use private houses and hostels. Today, the College retains much of its excellent medieval architecture.

Merton's ghosts are equally venerable: Duns Scotus (1266-1308) walks the Old Library, along with the founder of the University's Bodleian Library, Sir Thomas Bodley. There was a certain room in the college which could never be slept in, the reasons for this being lost, and was eventually made part of the library.

Jan Morris mentions an occasional visit from a serious young undergraduate ghost, dressed in clothes which date him to about the time of the First World War, who darts round Merton carrying a notebook. His identity and mission remain a mystery.

Merton's own local historian, Anthony Wood, who was born and died on Merton premises, writes of a ghost who appeared there in 1664, when:

"In the month of Jan. my friend Mr RL told me, as he was cutting up a calf's head on a Sunday morning, about 8 of the clock in his study, his dore stodd so much open that he might thrust his fist through, and hearing a russelling in his chamber, looked through that open space of his doore, and saw the appearance of a beautifull yonge man with long flaxen haire to his middle and a silke studying gowne on: and going to his study doore and oping it asked "Who is there, Sir John?" (meaning Sir John Hales who was his opposite neighbour) and going out into his chamber and seeing noe body, looked in his other study and none there either. Then he went to his chamber doore and that was shut and lached and could not be opened and shut without noise. And opeing the doore Sir John Hales came out of his owne, who (i.e. RL) asked him whether he was in his chamber, who (i.e. J.H.) answered faithfully that he was not. Whereupon he took this to be an appearance.'

New College, Holywell Street, was founded in 1379 by William of Wykeham, who also founded Winchester, the public school. The official name of the college is St Mary College of Winchester in Oxford, but as there was already a St Mary's College in existence - it later became known as Oriel the second St Mary's is always referred to as New College, not just 'New'. The original entrance to the college is hidden away down **New College Lane**, a medieval thoroughfare which Max Beerbohm described as a 'grim ravine', but loved by many for its twists and turns, its corbels, gargoyles and grotesques which combine to give it an other worldly atmosphere. The Lane is said to be haunted, some say by a spectral coach and horses which thunder along its length, as mentioned in Isis, 5th June 1968, but others insist that the ghostly hoof beats are those of a troop of Prince Rupert's cavalry setting out again at the dead of night to ambush a Parliamentarian pay train on its way over Shotover en route for London. Maybe they are heading for that field, just outside the village of Chalgrove, where John Hampden fought his last battle, managing to drag himself as far as Thame, where he died.

So well was William of Wykeham's design for New College carried out that very few alterations have been required in the college's six centuries. It presents a very pleasing and compact aspect, all the more surprising when one remembers that it was built on the site of a piece of waste ground which served as a rubbish tip.

The Bell Tower, which dates from 1400, is well known for its 'gargoyles', in reality grotesques carved with humorous and very human faces.

The ante-chapel houses an unusual statue, Epstein's *Lazarus* (1951), wrapped in grave clothes like a mummy. The chapel itself dates from 1386, and is well worth a visit for its stalls with their carved misericords, the founder's gold and enamel crosier, and the Nativity window designed by Reynolds, in which the artist himself appears as a shepherd.

This lovely chapel would appear to be haunted. One evening in 1962, a music lecturer at New College was alone there, clearing away after a late rehearsal. As an organist Dr DL was more than accustomed to being alone in dark and deserted buildings, and was less nervous than most. Eventually, he turned off the lights and was making his way in the darkness towards the exit at the far end of the chapel, After he had gone a few steps, however, something told him to turn round, and when he did so he saw, from a range of less than five feet, a man's white face above the Warden's stall.

"It was not a blur of light,' insisted Dr L, "but a definite face with all normal features the body must have been dark because it was not visible in the pitch darkness of the chapel. I assumed it was in academic or priestly dress. I turned away and walked for a few paces. Then I realised what I had seen and I ran all the way out of the chapel. I was terrified and since that

New College Lane

time I have never stayed alone in the chapel after dark. Some of the college members have tried to persuade me that what I saw was the ghost of Warden Spooner, whose description tallied with what I saw. I do not know who it was and I have no rational explanation for it."

Dr WA Spooner, who is credited with a great number of Spoonerism, some genuine, some contrived, was Warden from 1903 to 1924, and the white face above the Warden's stall could be explained by the fact that he was an albino.

A feature on **The Playhouse Theatre**, Beaumont Street, appeared in the *Oxford Journal*, in April 1978. A cleaning lady, Mrs FD, was collecting her equipment from the basement at 8.30 one morning, when a white lady suddenly floated through the wall of the cellar-like room. This is considerably older than the theatre itself which was only built in the 1930's. The lady drifted past the astonished Mrs D, and then vanished through the bricks of the wall opposite.

This was not the first sighting of the white lady, and so the Playhouse staff decided to do some detective work. They found out that the present building is thought to occupy the site of a Carmelite monastery. Carmelites were known as White Friars from the colour of the cloaks which they wore.

Although Mrs D was emphatic about the fact that the ghost wore a veil, it is possible that, in her shocked state, she assumed that it was wearing female clothing, rather than a cloak or robe.

The theatre staff also found out that when there was a Carmelite monastry on the Playhouse site, it had included a monks' burial ground which had since been disturbed.

The Sheldonian Theatre, in Broad Street, is Sir Christopher Wren's first major building. Opened in 1669, it is the venue for all University ceremonies, as well as being Oxford's leading concert hall.

One afternoon in 1984, the Assistant Custodian arrived in the empty building well before her starting time of 2 p.m. She locked the door behind her and, on going into the main section of the Theatre, noticed immediately that one of the two large, heavy prints that hung on either side of a doorway was missing. Its partner hung there looking very forlorn and lopsided. She searched for it and, when unable to find it, assumed that the

Sheldonian Theatre during a Degree Ceremony

glass had been broken or that it had been taken off to have some other repair done. She then made herself a coffee and went downstairs to the toilet. On her return, the first thing that caught her eye was the missing picture, hanging innocently in its usual place.

Several months later, the entire Theatre was being rewired. One of the electricians asked if the building had a ghost, but was very unwilling to reveal his reasons for asking. When pressed, all he would say was that he was "fed up with being watched!" From that time he refused to either work downstairs in the basement or be drawn into further conversation on the matter.

Weeks passed and then the Assistant Custodian, who was returning down the 114 steps from the Cupola after having checked the windows at closing time. She was surprised to hear the Custodian's voice calling out, "Are you all right?" as he hurried along the corridor to meet her.

She replied that she was fine, and wondered why he had asked such a question.

"Why did you shout, Brian! Brian! then?" asked the Custodian.

She assured him that she had not said a word and, furthermore, had not heard anything herself. At this, he was disconcerted and a little sheepish, but cheered up on being thanked for his chivalrous action.

Several days later, when he himself was in the Theatre alone, he was near the doorway where the picture hung. As he turned to face the doorway, his attention was drawn to the white frilly hem of a dress or petticoat which swished round the door at ground level.

Months passed without anything else of that nature happening. Then footsteps were heard in the corridors by different members of staff when the building was locked and empty, usually about 11 at night after a concert. Twice, untraceable blue flashes were seen, once outside in the Quad, and once in the locked Upper Gallery; both times the building was empty.

After a lapse of years, the Assistant Custodian was in the Ladies toilets, in the basement, at the bottom of a flight of steps. She had just left a cubicle when she heard the sound of light, swift footsteps running down the stairs, and the unmistakable sound of the outer door banging on its hinges. She waited to see who the newcomer would be. No one.

About a year later, she was with the Custodian, (not Brian, but his successor) in a basement storeroom near the bottom of this same flight of steps. They knew that they were alone, and were surprised to hear what sounded like a young girl running down the stairs. It was exactly the same sound as before. They rushed out to confront the intruder, but, as before, no one.

There is no mention in the Theatre's extensive records to give any clue as to what has been heard there, neither has anyone been able to come up with any suggestions. A new fire alarm system will shortly be installed in the building, and this time the Sheldonian staff will be prepared well in advance for any mysterious sights and sounds.

The richest college in Oxford, **St John's College**, in St Giles' Street is also one of the most prestigious academically. It was founded in 1555 by Sir Thomas White, Lord Mayor of London, on the site of the Cistercian College of St Bernard, itself built in 1437 by order of Archbishop Chichele, founder of All Souls College.

In the chapel lie the founder, Archbishop Juxon, a former College President who attended Charles I on the scaffold, and Archbishop Laud, another President, who was himself beheaded in 1645. The Oxford historian, Anthony Wood of Merton, describes Laud's second burial. He had first been interred in the church of All Hallow, Barking, but, after the restoration of Charles II, St John's obtained permission for him to be brought to Oxford in 1663.

"The day then, or rather night, being appointed wherein he should come to Oxfordshire, most of the Fellows, about 16 or 20 in number, went to meet him towards Whately; and after they had meet him about 7 of the clock on Friday July 24, 1663, they came into Oxon at 10 at night, and with the said number before him, and his corps (laying in a hors litter on 4 wheels drawn by 4 horses) following, and a coach after that. In the same manner they went up to St Marie's church; then up Cat Street; then to the back doore of St John's grove, where taking the coffin out conveyed to the chappell; and when Mr George Gisbey, fellow of that house and vice-president, had spoken a speech, they laid him, inclosed in a wooden coffin, in a littel vault at the upper end of the chancell between the founder's and Archbishop Juxon's. The next day following they hung up 7 streamers."

In spite of, or maybe because of, all this activity, Laud is reputed to extricate himself from his 'little vault' and come across to the library, there to enact one of the best known and least authenticated of all Oxford hauntings. What Oxford child has not heard the tale of how the Archbishop plays bowls with Charles I, along the length of the library floor, using their own severed heads. How does he manage to aim, and what is his success rate? Unfortunately there does not seem to be any recorded account of this haunting, the only detail we have being that they make their way along the former level of the floorboards, altered since their time. (reported in *Isis*, 5th June 1968).

Trinity College, in Broad Street, was founded in 1555 by Sir Thomas Pope, Privy Councillor to Henry VIII, and close friend to Sir Thomas More. The original buildings were erected on the site of Durham College, founded in 1286 for Benedictine monks from the monastery at Durham, and suppressed in 1544. A good deal of it was incorporated into that part of Trinity which is now called Durham Quad.

The hauntings take place in the College chapel which stands to the south of Durham Quad and is flanked by a medieval library and the seventeenth-century hall. The chapel was built in the 1690's and is known for its painted and stuccoed ceiling and finely carved woodwork, accredited to Grinling Gibbons.

In 1966, the organ was rebuilt by the generosity of Sir Harry Brittain. A celebratory service was held but, at the end of the first hymn, the congregation heard 'a curious off-key wailing sound.' During the reading, the Dean crept along to investigate and found that the organist was sprawled out dead across the console having suffered a fatal heart attack. This tragedy triggered off rumours of an evil ghost's being at large in the chapel.

A more substantiated haunting was that witnessed by the Verger, Mr H. The year was 1959 and, one sunny morning, as was his habit, he unlocked the chapel door and went inside to dust the pews. Just at 10 o'clock, his attention was drawn by something which told him to look to his right. When he did so, he saw a lady standing about ten feet away from him. She was dressed entirely in black and was smiling at him. This is the account which he gave to *Isis*, 5th June 1968:

"There was nothing at all ghostly about the figure; at first I thought it was a real person, but as I looked I realised that it couldn't be - I had just unlocked the chapel doors. Her body was simply black and it was her face which I gazed at. It was beautiful and smiling and I could see every detail.

We both stood still and I looked at her for about a minute and all the time she smiled. I started to move a pace or two nearer and looked down at the first step to the pews, taking my eyes off her for a second. When I

Trinity College chapel

looked up again there was nothing but the empty chapel.

I was overcome by the experience and, as I calmed down, I was aware of the nagging feeling that I half-recognised the figure. Although it did not look like anyone I had ever known, I recognised its features and manner in some odd way. When I got back to my house I looked on the mantelpiece at a photograph of my dead mother, and I suddenly realised who the figure was."

Wadham College, in Parks Road, was founded by Nicholas and Dorothy Wadham, but, as Nicholas died in 1609 before the college was established, his widow is credited with being the true founder in 1612. Wadham was built on the site of an Augustinian friary which Dorothy had bought in 1610 from the Oxford Corporation. The range of buildings which she erected were so well planned that there was little need for alteration until the twentieth century.

When the present chapel was being built, a number of skeletons, presumably of friars, were discovered under a series of numbered paving slabs. These are still clearly visible in the chapel, seemingly where the skeletons were reburied, forming a strange pattern with the streaks and swirls of light which fall on them through the stained glass in the windows.

One of the Wadham legends features a white monk who walks from the chapel doorway, across Front Quad, up the steps into Hall, and then along to high table where he vanishes.

In the winter of 1964, Mr AR, the Head Porter, was carrying out his usual security check shortly before midnight, and had just left the Hall. He was making his way towards No 4 Staircase, when, as he told Isis, 5th June 1968:

"Some instinct made me turn round and look towards the big double doors of the chapel. There, standing in front of me was a white figure looking at me. It was robed and seemed to be wearing a cowl. It was either a priest or a woman. It was definitely a human figure, although a little cloudy. I suppose it was about six foot tall and appeared to be looking my way. I was not afraid at all and moved on to Staircase 5, where I looked round again to find that the figure was gone. I was not tired at all because I hadn't been working during the day, and I certainly wasn't expecting to see a ghost."

Wadham College, Front Quad

29

In June 1967, Mr C, a scout at Wadham, was clearing away after late dinner at High Table. It was about 11.30 p.m., and there were three scouts engaged in this way. Just as he was leaving the Hall Mr C turned round, as if on impulse, and saw a grey figure, robed and cowled, standing near the fireplace.

"I thought I was seeing things until I looked again. It was definitely a human figure, and the other scouts saw it too. It was about six feet tall and looked like a priest. After a few seconds, the figure vanished and I was staring into the empty Hall. I heard footsteps and I beat it quickly out of the Hall. If I saw it again I'd stick around and study it.

I've been here nine years and I've never heard of a ghost in Wadham before."

A third account of the ghost was given by Mr EW, a scout on Staircase 15, who saw precisely the same figure, in the same place, and whose description of it tallies exactly with that of Mr CS.

Yet another member of the Wadham staff to have experienced it is Mr MH, Head Steward in the 1960's, who had then been in the College's employ for more than twenty years. He explained,

"I have been in my office quite late at night on many occasions, and heard footsteps in the Hall, directly above my office. The footsteps have walked down the Hall, but I've never heard them going back. Many times I've dashed up there only to find the Hall deserted. I've never seen the ghost. The footsteps stop directly above my room."

Mr H's room was situated exactly under the spot where at least three people have seen the ghostly monk, and in addition to Mr H's testimony, his colleague, the Head Chef at the time also heard the footsteps coming from above the Steward's Office while the two men were there late at night. Neither of the witnesses was in contact with the others in any way as regards their accounts, nor can anyone come up with any conclusion other than that Wadham has a well-authenticated resident monk.

CHAPTER TWO:
THE GREATER OXFORD AREA

*Tourist Information Centre, 15-16 Broad Street, Oxford OX1 2DA.
Tel: 01865 726871*

Barton Estate, lying to the east of the city, beyond Headington proper, off the A40, is a large housing development. It was started in 1946 for rehousing those families whose homes were to be demolished in the replanning of the shabby working-class district of St Ebbe's, in the city centre. Barton sprawls down from the main road into a valley, almost to the edge of Otmoor.

The ancient settlement of Barton, as opposed to the housing estate, derives its name from an enclosure where barley was grown, or from a farmyard; it lies well away from the A40, to the north of the estate. It is a very ancient settlement, although today it consists of little more than Wick Farm with its Roman bath in the middle of the farmyard. This is thought to be the only example of a stone-roofed bath to exist in this country.

In the autumn of 1981, Wick Farm suddenly hit the local headlines as the haunt of Nellie (or Nannie) Martin. The *Oxford Star*, 1st October 1981, received a letter requesting information about Nellie's story, as the writer had apparently seen a ghost in the vicinity of the crematorium, about two fields away from Wick Farm. Several readers responded with accounts of Nellie's life, demise and possible afterlife.

One of the most detailed stories relates how Nellie, a servant girl at this remote place, gave birth to a child - presumably illegitimate - and drowned it in the Roman bath one stormy winter's night. She then set off across the fields, only to sink into a bog, not far from the farm. Because of the wildness of the night, her cries for help went unheard, and in her weakened condition, she quickly died of exposure. Several letters told of the time that a young man, a little the worse for drink, attempted to waylay Nellie as she walked. When he tried to steal a kiss, she melted in his arms.

The matter of fact way that these letters were composed, proved that Nellie occupies a very real place in the history of the area.

Also in the Barton area, a very large black dog, some say about the size of a donkey, pads silently along. He may well be a relative of the Black Suck of Eastern England, a giant animal with eyes like coach lamps, which we have inherited from our Viking ancestors, for he is one of Odin's hounds. Part of his beat, Ashot, is one of those ancient pathways along which, according to local lore, the carrying of a corpse will ensure a right of way.

A phantom rider is a much more frequent and well-documented visitor, and has been around for many years. An Australian lady became friendly with an English couple and, when she learned that they had a friend living in Headington, told them about an experience which her husband had had there, and asked if they would get their friend to make enquiries in the area.

This happened in 1979, when the husband was working as a sales representative in the Oxford area. He was driving along the A40, just past the roundabout leading to Barton Estate, when a phantom horseman suddenly appeared on a white horse, jumped over a hedge, and then vanished. The first time that this happened he didn't like to tell his wife as he feared that he was either over-tired or 'going potty', as he put it. The second time an identical thing happened he did tell her, and when it happened a third time, she was extremely interested. Shortly after this, though, they emigrated to Australia, and so she had little chance to investigate.

Blackbird Leys housing estate stretches out beyond Cowley. Started in 1957, this development would not be the obvious place for a haunting, but in the 1980's, in a house on Blackbird Leys, a 'very sweet-looking lady' was seen on numerous occasions by all the members of the B family, between 1962 and about 1970. The lady was always seen in the vicinity of a certain chair, given to the family by Mr B's mother in 1958, and much loved by one of the young sons of the house.

"It was an old invalid-type chair which adjusted to a bed, probably Victorian," relates Mrs B, "but my husband thinks more 1910-20. Eventually this chair stood in one corner of our bedroom, and our daughter would never go into that room, although she didn't know why -

she would flatly refuse to fetch things from the airing cupboard, saying she didn't like our room, and would hesitate to pass if the door was open! Strangely, we often had the feeling that someone was in the house and so that the children wouldn't be afraid, we made jokes about `dear Clarence', so when a door slammed or a curtain moved, they would say, `Oh, it's only Clarence.'

Then, one night while my husband was on night shift, Sally, our dog, who slept at the top of the stairs, began howling - and I mean howling! Suddenly, she sat bolt upright and stared, ears pricked, into the dark corners of the room. I looked to see what she was looking at, and, to my astonishment, standing right through the centre of the `bed-chair' was a lady. She was about 30-35, short fair, close-waved hair, and a grey dress (which, I suppose, could have been blue in that light). It had a square neck and elbow-length, puffed sleeves; I couldn't see if it was long because the lower half of her was hidden by the seat of the chair. She had the sweetest face, and was looking directly at me, smiling. The most amazing thing of all was I was not afraid. In fact my first thought was, `What is she doing here?' I stared, and Sally stared, and gradually she faded. Then I thought, `Oh, my God! ` I turned over away from the chair and immediately felt an ice-cold draught across my ear and cheek. I told my husband the next morning, and he said, `Say nothing to the kids.'

The next evening we went to visit my sister . . . I said to her, `Guess what happened last night, I had the strangest experience during the night.' and believe it or not, she said, `I bet you saw a lady.' When she saw my face, she said, `Fair hair and wearing a grey dress?'

You can imagine, I went cold. `How did you know?'

`Because Dallas (our daughter) saw her months ago, on the landing, and told me not to tell you in case you were afraid!'

I was dumbfounded, as you can imagine. Then, to cap it all, we were watching a programme about a haunted church, and our younger son said, `I've seen a ghost.'

Now, my husband and I were very interested as we had said nothing to the children, and neither had my sister who was sworn to secrecy.

My son told us that one night, while asleep in bed, he was awakened by something, and it couldn't be me because she had fair hair. He also said that he was not afraid because she looked so kind, and so he just went back to sleep. Thinking about it, he realised that it must have been a ghost, so said nothing in case we thought he was silly.

This really got me thinking, so I told my husband to get rid of the chair and, to be absolutely sure, he burnt it. Since then, no one has seen or heard anything as far as I know, and it was only two years ago that we got together and the whole fascinating puzzle fitted together."

Sometimes Mrs B wishes that the chair had not been destroyed so that she might have another chance to speak to the sweet faced lady in grey.

Cowley, which lies mainly within the city boundary, about 2½ miles south east of the city centre, derives its name from the Saxon for `Cufa's clearing', and is mentioned in the Domesday survey of 1086, by which time it was a well established community.

The Norman St James' church and a few old houses remain, but nothing else much in Cowley is ancient. Its claim to fame is as the birthplace of William Morris, later Lord Nuffield, and the home of his motor works, under all their subsequent titles. Morris's original workshop, where he started making bicycles but later changed over to making cars, is in Longwall Street, in the city, but he transferred his premises to Cowley and began work in the former Military College there.

Cowley Barracks used to be haunted by a phantom soldier. Sited on the former Bullingdon Green, on the borders of Cowley and Headington, they were built in 1877 as a depot for the 43rd and 52nd Foot Regiments of the Oxfordshire and Buckinghamshire Light Infantry. In its heyday, the complex consisted of a keep, canteen, hospital, officers' and married quarters, and of course accommodation for the men themselves. The barracks have had a varied career since they ceased to be used for military purposes, when they were converted into housing for homeless families, it was suggested that the ghost might have found himself in need of another home.

Among the local people who insist that the site is haunted, was the champion Oxford letter-writer, Raymond Cantwell, who met the ghost while stationed at Cowley Barracks during his (Mr Cantwell's) service with the Royal Army Medical Corps.

It is that of a shadowy soldier, dressed in old-fashioned uniform, and his favourite haunt was the tower. He would stand there rather forlornly, just gazing around him, as if he were considering whether to jump off. No one has any suitable ideas as to his identity, what uniform he wore, or even what his rank was. No doubt some tragedy lies behind his appearance on the tower.

On 16th April 1971, the *Oxford Mail* produced a feature on the Barracks ghost. At this time it had just been announced that the tower was scheduled for demolition later that year. The newspaper appealed for any information which would help to identify the phantom soldier in any way, and to find out if he did indeed commit suicide by leaping to his death there. No satisfactory conclusion was reached.

Divinity Road runs from cosmopolitan Cowley Road nearly up to Oxford Brookes University at Headington. The properties in the road vary considerably in age, size and the condition in which they are maintained, but the majority are divided up into flats or bed sits and are no longer private houses.

When Mr and Mrs Y moved into their room in an Edwardian house in this road, the colleague from work who already lived there mentioned that it was supposed to be haunted. She had never seen or heard anything suspect herself, but the previous occupant of their room had complained of unexplained footsteps on the stairs which stopped suddenly just outside the room.

A couple of weeks later, Mrs Y was at her parents' house, when her Turkish-speaking husband rang her from home. He sounded distressed and kept repeating that the house had hayalet. As Mrs Y had no idea what this was, she was not particularly worried about it, although it did not sound very pleasant. Dry rot? Wet rot? Blocked drains? Well, she would find out soon enough when she got back, she told herself. When she reached the house, she found him still upset; he thrust a dictionary into her hand and she then discovered that he was telling her that the house came complete with ghost.

Apparently, when he got home from work, he heard the front door open. This door made a very distinctive sound as it stuck, and had to be forced open to its full extent. He then heard feet coming upstairs and, when they stopped immediately outside the door of their room, he flung the door open, only to find nothing. No one was on the landing, the stairs, or in the doorway, neither had the footsteps gone back down again. The house was empty, the other occupants being still at work, and their rooms locked.

They settled down after this scare until, one evening, a large carving knife went missing. This knife was always kept in the same place, in a high cupboard, along with other cutlery which was in everyday use. Mrs Y got up onto a chair to see to the back of the shelf, but there was nothing to be found there. Not liking the idea of a knife of such size and sharpness being mislaid, they hunted for it all over the room, even pulling the bed away from the wall in a desperate search behind it. The rooms in the house were always kept locked, so anyone borrowing it was out of the question, even if they had known where it was hidden. The search was extended to the shared kitchen with a similar lack of success.

The Y's gave up on the knife after a couple of days, then, almost as if it had heard them and had had enough of playing hide-and-seek, the knife reappeared as suddenly as it had vanished. Mr Y put his hand up one morning for a spoon, and there it was, in its usual place, on top of the other cutlery, all of which had been used during its absence.

This was not the end of self-motivating items, however. One lunchtime, Mr Y had ironed his best trousers and had placed them carefully over the arm of a chair to prevent the appearance of unauthorised creases. He then set off for the bathroom, which was immediately next to their room. While he was in the bath, his wife went along to her friend's room, where they stood in the doorway, chattering about nothing in particular. This doorway was in full view of both the bathroom and the Ys' room, and they were facing these doors all the time that they were in conversation. They therefore saw and heard Mr Y as he made his way out of the bathroom and back to his own room. They also heard the shouts of rage which he gave when he discovered that his lovely clean trousers were missing from over the arm of the chair. They were not even in the room, so where on earth were they? The two women naturally denied all knowledge of what had happened to them, and hurried along to see for themselves.

The great trouser hunt began and was soon over. Another great roar came from the kitchen, where Mr Y had become reunited with his trousers, but not in the same condition as when he had last seen them.

They were lying on the kitchen floor, which, as in the case of most shared houses, left a little to be desired. No longer were they neatly pressed and folded, they were sitting there forming little wrinkled tunnels, one made from each leg, with the floor showing through at the bottom, just as if someone had just stepped out of them and walked away. No one could possibly have placed them like that without having worn them. The three of them tried for some time to recreate this effect, but neither of them could manage it.

Divinity Road

At the northern end of Port Meadow (qv), just outside Wolvercote, but on the far bank, stand the ruins of **Godstow Nunnery**. It was founded in 1133 and its large church was dedicated in 1139 in the presence of King Stephen. All that survives is the enclosing wall and the shell of the fifteenth-century chapel.

The Oxford historian Antony Wood, relates a charming story concerning the nunnery and its royal visitors:

> In the church of the nunnery of Godstow . . . was buried Rosamund, who died before her father, Walter, Lord Clifford. Rosamund. . . was in the flour of her youth concubine to King Henry II and afterwards a nun here. Over whose grave was this written:
> *Hic jacet in tumba Rosa mundi non rosa munda,*
> *Non redolet sed olet, quae redolere solet,*

which Wood summarises as `Here lyethe in grave Rose of the world, but not clene rose'.

He then quotes a fifteeenth-century author who gives a potted biography of Fair Rosamund, as she is usually known.

> *. . . in Englonde was a king that had a concubine whose name was Rose; and that for her great bewtye he cleped her Rose à monde, Rosa mundi, that is to saye, Rose of the world. For him thought that she passed al wymen in bewtye. It befel that she died and was buried while the king was absent. And whenne he Cambridge agen, for grete love that he had to yr, he wolde se the bodye in the grave and whan the grave was opened, there sate an orible tode upon hir breste bytwene hir teetys, and a fould adder birgirt hir body about in the midle. And she stanke so that the kyng, ne non other might stond to se that oryble sight. Than the kynge dyde shette agen the grave and did wryte these two veerses upon the grave: Hic Jacet, etc.*

The mighty bishop Hugh of Lincoln, who was visiting Godstow in 1191, was so appalled that a concubine should have such a fine and ornate tomb that he ordered her immediate eviction from the nunnery church, so that she had to reburied elsewhere.

Eventually, `her flesh being quite perished these chast sisters put all her bones in a perfumed leather bagge which bagge they enclosed in lead and layd them againe (with her stone coffin) in the church under a larg grave stone', writes Wood.

The nunnery was dissolved in 1539, and became a private house which was held for the King during the Civil War. Part of the nunnery ruins were made into fortifications, and, in 1645, the house was so badly damaged by fire that what remained was easily destroyed by Fairfax the following year.

Two girls, who had brought their caravan to Port Meadow and parked it in the nunnery grounds, asked an Oxford doctor and his daughter to stay up on watch with them one hot July night. The reason for this was because, on several previous nights, they had been disturbed by noises which suggested that a group of people had been prowling round outside their caravan. On the occasion that the father and daughter came to visit, nothing was heard, however, and so they went off to sleep while their hosts stayed awake on guard outside the caravan. A male undergraduate friend had come over from Oxford to keep them company.

About 4 in the morning, the girl woke her father up to tell him that the other three were standing just inside the chapel doorway, seemingly engrossed in watching something or somebody inside the ruined building. They did not attempt to investigate and afterwards the others came back without mentioning whatever it had been that they had been looking at inside the chapel.

When morning came, the student returned to Oxford immediately after breakfast. One of the girls then asked Dr C if, by any chance, he knew where the altar would have been in pre-Reformation times. At last, she revealed that, while the three of them had been on watch, they had suddenly been aware of a light which appeared in the ruined chapel. When they looked more closely, they had been able to make out a priest celebrating Mass in the building. In a statement to the *Oxford Mail,* the doctor quotes his informant as saying, `The altar lights were two enormous candles, the vestments were very beautiful and the early morning sun was shining through three lancet windows, two of which had long since been bricked up.' The three young people were not at all scared by what they were witnessing, and stayed watching the Mass until it faded away as suddenly as it had appeared. Later, Dr C took the opportunity of closely questioning the undergraduate as to what he had seen, and his description tallied exactly with that given by the girl.

Apart from the ghostly mass, there appear to be at least two other ghosts in the vicinity. According to an *Oxford Mail* report of August 1966, a couple of friends from Reading were living in a cabin cruiser moored on the riverbank at Godstow. About 11 o'clock one Friday night, they were strolling along the towpath above Godstow, on the far bank, when they happened upon a pair of ghosts. One took the form of a lady in a long flowing gown who kept bending down as if she were attempting to pick something up from the ground. The second was a male ghost wearing a hat with a turned-down brim and a short jacket. He, poor soul, 'tapered away below the knees'.

The two friends stood and watched for about ten minutes and, although the evening was dark and misty, the apparitions seemed to be luminous, and would vanish and reappear as if operated by some mysterious force. At last the watchers could stand it no longer, and shouted out, 'Who are you? What do you want?' but the only response was a sort of muttering. Neither of them cared to pursue the matter further and so they walked gingerly past the ghosts and on to their boat. When they reached home, they put on some cheerful music in a bid to calm themselves and bring back some reality into their thoughts.

Because the friends were not local - in fact one came from Jamaica - they had never heard anything about the nunnery's reputation for being haunted, and it was not until they related their experience to colleagues at work that they learned the story.

A couple of nights later, while his Jamaican friend was away for the weekend, the owner of the cruiser was treated to a repeat performance. This time the vision was less distinct than on the first occasion, but nevertheless he was easily able to recognise their radiant visitors.

Headington Hill leads from St Clement's up to Headington, and has public parks on either side of the road. The parish of St Clement stretches from Magdalen Tower to Marston Road, and the old parish church once stood where the roundabout at the Plain is now. In the 1820's, it was decided that this church was not large enough for the needs of the rapidly expanding population of the suburb and it was decreed that a new one be built. The present church was constructed in 1825, just into the Marston Road, at the bottom of the hill. It cost £6,500, most of which was raised by public subscription, contributors including Keble, Heber, and Sir Robert Peel. The new St Clement's church aroused considerable interest because it was the first church on a new site to be built in Oxford since the Reformation. The *Victoria County History* describes its style somewhat flatteringly as 'abortive Romanesque revival, inspired, it is said, by Iffley' - a masterpiece of genuine Norman craftsmanship - and goes on to state that the church's setting gained universal approval. St Clement's nickname, however, was 'the boiled rabbit', because it did not coincide with contemporary taste in architecture.

Just before the outbreak of the Great War, a man was cycling to work one morning at about 5.30. He was just approaching the junction of the Marston Road and St Clement's Street, when he became aware of a white figure which drifted in and out among the trees in the park which goes up the left side of Headington Hill. As he watched, fascinated, it glided over the stone wall which separates Marston Road from the park, crossed the road and made its way into St Clement's churchyard where it disappeared among the graves.

The park meets the grounds of Headington Hall on the brow of the hill. The Hall is now part of Oxford Brookes University, but previously housed both the Pergamon Press and the home of its owner, Robert Maxwell, who leased it from the City Council.

When the Maxwell family moved into 'the poshest council house in Oxford', they had great problems with the drains. The City Architect was called in and bravely struggled with the problem for eight long years with a singular lack of success. Isis, 5th June 1968, reports how, at the end of this period, he was forced to go to Mrs Maxwell and say that, sorry as he was, there was nothing further he could do to assist, as the entire house was 'founded on that drain, and you'd have to be a ghost to get down there and clear that.' Two days afterwards, the architect hanged himself. One the very night that he committed suicide, Headington Hall's drain suddenly and inexplicably righted itself, and has never given any trouble since.

One summer night in the early 1970's, two friends, Dave and Deidre, were walking home from Marlborough Road in Oxford to North Hinksey Lane and decided to take a cross country route via **Willow Walk**, setting off along the side of the canal, and via Osney Mead, where the industrial estate is now. They had made this journey several times before, by day and in the late evening, and knew the route well. They had spent the evening laughing, talking, playing music and having the odd glass of wine or beer. They left their friend's house about two in the morning and were looking forward to their stroll along the towpath in the stillness of the warm June night. By about three o'clock, they had nearly reached North Hinksey when they heard the sound of children's voices drifting across from a field near the river. They were both very surprised, and stopped still, looking at each other in silence. `I can hear kids playing, can't I?' asked Deidre, puzzled.

'Yes, I can!' Dave answered, `What on earth are they doing here? It's miles from anywhere. What time is it?'

'Just gone 3.15.' Deidre told him. 'But where are they? I can hear them clearly enough, so they can't be far away, but I can't see them anywhere.'

Then they looked all around them. The moon was almost full and the sky cloudless. Anybody as close as the shouting and laughter suggested must be clearly visible. There was nobody in sight however, although the sound of children's voices, raised in excitement as they played, remained as loud as ever.

'We'd better have a good look round.' Dave said worriedly, 'They can't be far away and there's obviously several of them. How old would you say they are, Dee?'

'Ten or eleven. Twelve at the most. Certainly too young to be out here in the middle of the night by themselves. What can their parents be thinking about!'

The pair worked their way towards the river bank, dreading to hear a splash any minute, but still unable to see anything or anybody. The laughter went on as if to mock them, although the children seemed unaware that they were not alone. Dave and Deidre called out to them, asking them to show themselves and to come away from the water, but there was no response. It was not long before they had made a thorough search of their immediate surroundings. They drew a blank and had to concede defeat; children there were none. By the time they had satisfied themselves of this, the sound had stopped, so they walked on towards North Hinksey Lane.

When they reached Deidre's house, they could not get the children's voices out of their thoughts, and kept discussing them. Then one of them hit on the idea of looking in the Radio Times to find out, if by some strange chance there had been a programme featuring children at play which had been broadcast that night. Of course, by that time the radio stations had either gone off the air for the night or were playing pop music. There had been nothing earlier in the evening that sounded at all likely to have been anything resembling what they had heard. So realistic had the voices been that it was not until the following day that they asked themselves why someone should have taken a transistor radio to such a remote spot, and then walked off and left it playing. In any case, why hadn't Dave or Deidre found it?

In the end, they were forced to come to the conclusion that they had been present at the start of a reinactment of some long-forgotten tragedy which had claimed the lives of several children at that particular stretch of Willow Walk where they had heard the ghost children happily at play.

There was, however, an eerie sequel to their experience. Later that same summer, Deidre's brother, Liam, was walking home along Willow Walk on a hot, still afternoon. As he approached the narrow stone bridge which it was necessary to cross in order to reach North Hinksey Lane, he became aware of a couple of men standing on the bridge, silently staring into the water. There was nothing strange about that, apart from the fact that they were dressed in full Puritan costume. Liam just assumed that they were either appearing in some period drama, a common enough occurrence in Oxford, or maybe members of the Sealed Knot Society taking a well earned rest between skirmishes. He didn't give the matter much thought at all until he started to cross the bridge and they made no attempt to get out of his way.

Liam said, 'Excuse me!' and waited for them to move. When they did not, but continued to stare morosely down over the parapet, he repeated his request. They still ignored him and took no notice of each other either. Annoyed at being treated as if he did not exist, Liam tried to edge past them and only then did he get a reaction. As he brushed against him, one of the men turned and silently placed his hand on Liam's wrist, as if to detain or reprimand him. Where the Puritan's fingers had touched his skin, Liam's wrist began to sting and he was aware of a burning sensation as if he had been in contact with acid or some other corrosive substance, He pushed them aside then and hurried home as fast as he could without breaking into a run, reasoning that if he showed signs of fear the mysterious men might give chase. He did not turn round to see what they were doing, or if they were still on the bridge.

Within a few hours the skin on Liam's wrist came up into an angry blister which remained several days; it was clearly visible a week after his experience, as his friends and family were able to testify.

Only two miles south east of Oxford on the banks of the Thames, **Iffley** is today a suburb, but nevertheless a place apart in many ways. This sense of isolation is part of the attraction of the heart of the old village, little affected by the housing developments virtually on its doorstep. Apart from recently built roads and closes, Iffley consists of one main street flanked by low stone houses and cottages, some thatched, and several dating back to the Middle Ages. One such building is the thatched school which started life as a barn and was promoted to the status of parish school in 1838; the Rectory contains thirteenth-century work and many other reminders of medieval craftsmen. It is St Mary's church which is its principal attraction featuring in travel books and architectural works, it is so well known. The chancel is believed to have been constructed out of a complete Saxon church and the entire building is a fine example of a Norman one, the doorways and windows being particularly noteworthy.

Iffley's main street, which stops abruptly at the church gates, is called Church Way and is the setting for an amusing haunting which took place at some unspecified date in the not too distant past. The ghost itself, presumed to be that of a sailor, has been well documented and was said to wear a large, soft hat and own a wooden leg, both of which gave a clue to its occupation. It took to roaming around the village late at night, making such a clatter and clump with its wooden stump, that it became a real nuisance to the residents of Iffley. When the villagers could stand it no longer, certain members of the local clergy were invited to take part in a service of exorcism in an attempt to rid the place of its phantom prowler. The reverend gentlemen, for reasons known only to themselves, declined the invitation.

Not deterred, the villagers looked round for someone to champion them in their struggle with the intruder and finally accepted an offer of help from a down-and-out who had once been in service with a naval chaplain. They assumed, not unnaturally, that he might have considerable experience, both with sailors and wooden legs, or perhaps they were just desperate. The evening before the nocturnal confrontation had been scheduled, the self-appointed ghost hunter was taken to a local hostelry, where he was plied with Dutch courage. The moment of truth arrived, as did the ghost, and the whole of Iffley held its breath as their champion lurched into action. Unfortunately, his technique was not of the best, in fact he was a disaster. He stood there, in the middle of Church Way, vainly attempting to keep his balance, while he waved a bicycle pump and got quite aggressive with those he was supposed to be protecting. In short, he proved much more of a nuisance than the poor old ghost himself, who could not prevent making such a row as he tapped his peg-leg along the road. In any case, there was no record of his ever having said a word out of place, let alone being threatening or abusive to anyone.

So unpleasant did the situation become that the police were called in; they carted the troublemaker away and booked him for being drunk and disorderly, leaving the ghost to have the last laugh.

To most Oxford residents, the **Minchery Farm Estate**, between Cowley and Littlemore, evokes a typical 1950's housing estate, with wide roads of modern houses and blocks of flats. However, the estate is on the site occupied by a small priory; according to the *Oxford Mail*, 28th June 1957, the name 'Minchery' is supposed to be derived from minchon, a nun. The priory was founded by the Benedictines in the early twelfth century, and taken over by the Templars; it was dissolved in 1525, after some reputed scandals came to light.

In 1955, two next door neighbours living in Priory Road on the estate were terrified to find a ghost on their doorsteps. Mrs J looked out of her window at three in the morning and '. . . saw the shadow of a person come up to the door of No 36. It moved so quickly I could not see whether it was a man or a woman but it was only about four feet tall. It seemed to float along.'

Much later, Mrs J found out that her neighbour, Mrs F, had had the same experience that night. She was terrified to see a ' . . .figure dressed in black' in the front garden.

'It came as far as next door and then floated back. It certainly wasn't a real person - a real person could not move so quickly.' She added that the figure was indeed only about 4 feet in height, and confessed that she had been too frightened to look out of the window on subsequent nights, and '. . . couldn't sleep for ages afterwards.'

Another neighbour, Mr R E, told the *Oxford Times* that on several evenings he had heard what he believed to be a bicycle freewheeling down Priory Road towards the bridge, but there was nothing to be seen. This bridge leads to Minchery Farm itself, a building which incorporates the remaining fabric of the nunnery.

New Marston stretches northeastwards from St Clement's, along Marston Road, until it joins up with Headington beyond Northway Estate. Much of New Marston is made up of that typically English style of housing which grew up between the wars, solid and respectable semis, with bow windows and neat little front gardens.

In just such a house, just off a main road leading into the city, lived the Simpkins family. They are convinced that the house is still occupied by the spirit of their little grandson, Troy, who died there in the 1970's at the age of five, after being accidentally knocked on the head by a friend at play. Troy spent all of his short life at his grandparents' house, where he lived with his mother. He was a friendly, intelligent boy, old beyond his years as only children often are. He was particularly fond of animals, his best friend being the family cat. He also enjoyed talking to people, and, like most small boys, playing tricks.

Mr and Mrs Simpkins kept a framed photograph of Troy on a table in their front room, and on top of the frame, its legs dangling over his portrait, sat Troy's favourite toy monkey. Apparently, it is of the utmost importance that the monkey stay in its proper place; if it is moved elsewhere for any reason, every other ornament on the table, and there are plenty of them, will be moved around until the monkey returns to his picture frame.

Mr Simpkins had an experience with a broken musical box which was kept on top of a wardrobe, with other items stored on top of it. It should play when the lid is raised, yet during the night, although broken and weighted down, it used to sometimes play of its own accord. Similarly, an old radio from which the batteries had been removed, also on top of the wardrobe, suddenly started playing music one morning.

The kitchen seemed to be another focus for Troy's attentions. The bread bin lid was seen to flap up and down, like the upper part of a set of dentures, and one day the unfortunate cat was nearly scared witless by a saucepan which leaped into the air and followed it.

Perhaps the most unusual happening was when the teapot left its shelf, travelled through the air, and disappeared out of the kitchen door, still sailing sedately upright. It was recovered from the shared driveway, upright and undamaged. Just as the neighbour's son was returning home on his moped, it took flight; unfortunately, the young man had just recovered from a sort of breakdown, and all this proved too much for him. Very disturbed by the queer goings on next door', the family moved away shortly afterwards.

Another neighbour who was also annoyed by the happenings was a woman from along the road who had been less than kind to Mrs Simpkin's mother when she was living with them. After the old lady died, her belongings, much of them of good quality, including some china, were stored for safekeeping in a cupboard. On several occasions, the unwelcome neighbour was greeted with the cupboard door bursting open and its contents being disgorged onto the floor. After this had happened several times, the woman took the hint and stayed away.

The Simpkins were not at all distressed by the visitations; Troy had never wanted for anything while alive, and seemed to be happily revisiting his old surroundings.

Northway Estate, which joins Headington to Marston, was started in the1950's. The haunted site is in Marston and the house concerned backs onto a very large field, full of trees and ditches. The only thing that divided the house from this field was a wire mesh fence at the bottom of the garden.

In about 1981, Miss D, who no longer lives in the area and does not wishes to disclose the identity of the property, gave the following account of her experience there:

"This particular evening I was returning home via the back entrance to the house. After passing through the gate, I saw this peculiar sight right over the other side of the field about 700 to 1000 yards away. It was a lady with long blonde hair, in a very glowing white dress, (in fact the dress was dazzling), and carrying a large, brown package in front of her, supporting this with both her hands. She was walking straight towards me and this was just so amazing as she was walking through trees, ditches, etc., and, although she only seemed to be walking at a moderate speed, it was very, very fast. Within only a few seconds, she was standing at the bottom of the garden, behind the fence, for a split second, then, to my absolute amazement, she walked through the fence and went behind the willow tree that was at the bottom of the garden, actually in my parents' property. I stood there for a few minutes, just watching, but I saw nothing, so I started walking down the garden to look behind the tree. There was nothing at all there, no trace of this glowing lady. I was just so shocked, in fact I couldn't believe what I had seen. But she was there. I'm absolutely sure of that to this day. After this, I went inside the house and told my mother, and to her, I suppose, it sounded even more strange, but I do think that she believes me, as I was just so shocked about it. I never saw her (i.e.) the lady again after that, as we moved to Cowley, but I will never forget it. I wish I knew what it was, it must have been something supernatural as she was so glowing, in fact outstanding."

To the north west of the city, between the Isis and the railway, is **Port Meadow**, 400-odd acres of meadowland. The Meadow has belonged to the Freemen of Oxford since early medieval times and they guard their privileges jealously. One of these is the entitlement to keep their horses and ponies there; the animals have to be registered in order to graze there and, once a year on an unspecified date, the Sheriff rounds them all up and impounds them in a surprise raid. They are released on receipt of a statutory payment and any illegal grazers incur a fine. This custom was started in 1834, prior to which the roundup was carried out by bailiffs. Equine tenants share the Meadow with geese, ducks, cows, yachts, campers, bathers and ghosts. At some times of the year the Meadow gives the impression of being situated at the edge of the world, when all that is visible of Oxford is one or two towers and spires peeping eerily through the mist or fog. Remote as it seems, however, Port Meadow has seen one or two important incidents, such as Charles I's escape from Oxford with his troops, the same Royalists who appear in phantom form on 3rd June near Yarnton.

Port Meadow was used as an airfield during the Great War, and a plaque on the bridge near Godstow commemorates two airmen who lost their lives in a crash near the spot. An employee of Lucy's Iron Foundry in Walton Well Road, was walking along the road, near the bridge over the railway, when he met another man coming towards him. He did not take much notice of the stranger as he approached, and the two passed each other with barely a glance. As soon as the other man had gone by, however, something prompted him to turn round to have a second look, for it had just dawned on him that the second man was dressed in a flying suit, somewhat conspicuous in this part of Oxford. As he turned round, however, the aviator vanished completely.

In the summer of 1971, a group of students from the College of Further Education was having a barbecue, nearly opposite the Perch, on the Oxford side of the river. They were there to celebrate the end of `A' level examinations and about twenty of them were gathered on the riverbank. They made a huge bonfire, roasted some potatoes in their jackets, cooked some sausages, and opened up cans of beer and soft drinks. There was nothing at all eerie about the spot they had chosen; they were in full view of anything and anybody and were having what amounted to a farewell party. Although there was some beer, there was certainly no spirits and definitely no drugs of any kind This needs to be emphasised as this was the era of flower power, and such things were by no means unknown. The atmosphere there on the bank was cheerful, everybody was relaxed as they knew and liked each other. Furthermore, it was a beautiful clear night and they could see right across to the Perch, a distance of several hundred yards.

After a couple of hours, they were joined by two other students who were stopping off in Oxford en route for interviews at the Royal College of Music in London. They had guitars with them and soon everyone was joining in the singing, students and lecturers alike. The conversation was mainly about college and student life in general. This went on long after the pubs had closed, and they had been able to see revellers returning from the Perch public house, opposite. Suddenly, a figure was evident on the far bank, about a field away from where they were sitting. It came into view without actually arriving. They became aware of it in twos and threes, but at first no one said a word. The figure moved along with no up and down movement, indeed its progress was unnaturally even, and its appearance gave no indication of light or dark parts which might suggest a face, hair or clothing. It was uniformly grey, little more than a filled-in outline, with no features or limbs, just the head and shoulders being defined. The watchers were particularly conscious of its height, which must have been about 8 feet by comparison with the people whom they had seen earlier in the evening from approximately the same distance away. It towered above the cows as it made its stately way past them. Soon the entire group had become aware of it, whatever it was, and they had all risen to their feet, watching and waiting to see what would happen next. They then plucked up courage to tell each other what they could see, and all of the descriptions tallied. In fact, the situation was not at all scary; they were more fascinated and anxious not to frighten the figure away. They stood spellbound for about two full minutes. At last, one of their number - he later became ordained - held out his arms in the shape of a cross and called out, 'I'll cross it through it blast me!' in true Shakespearean fashion.

At this, the visitor looked as surprised as any faceless thing can manage to do, and stopped dead in its tracks. It remained thus for several seconds and gave the impression of staring in their direction, as if deciding what to do next. Unfortunately, it was not as persistent as Hamlet's father and moved off again, only to disintegrate, so that after about fifteen seconds or so there was nothing to indicate where it had been. The party stared across at where it had been, and then someone thought to look at the time. It was 12.05 a.m. They had been so engrossed that they had failed to notice that a couple had joined them some minutes previously. The boy asked, 'So, you've seen it too, then?'

The students feigned ignorance and asked him to explain what he was talking about. He told them that his brother had seen something identical to what they had just witnessed earlier that week.

Two or three nights later, one of the youngsters who had been on Port Meadow said, 'I wonder what the date was the night we had the barbecue, and if there's any connection with what we saw?' When they worked it out, they realised it had been 23rd June, Midsummer's Eve.

Nearly a decade later, on an autumn evening in 1980, two girls were driving through Wolvercote on their way to the Trout at Godstow for a drink. It was an exceptionally quiet weekday evening, and the driver was struck by the fact that there was virtually no traffic on the road. They had got as far as a narrow stretch of road where there was no opportunity to overtake: on their right was a raised path and a hedge, on the left trees, among which played a gloomy, yellowish light. The girl who was driving was thinking how the passages between the trees made her think of pictures she had seen of alleyways in the East End slums at the period when Jack the Ripper was at large. Then, suddenly, without any warning, out stepped, or floated, a grey and shadowy figure. It came so close to the car that it could not be seen below thigh level, and it could not be further identified, beyond being just a 'thing'. It seemed to be clad in some sort of cloak, but did not look like a man, because, in some inexplicable way, its shape did not resemble a male. It was more like a half-sideways silhouette, with no discernible features and, although it was not opaque, it was not transparent either, being like a thick veil. As the apparition became clearer, the driver slammed on the brakes to avoid running into it. Then it just disappeared, 'Now you see it, now you don't.'

The two friends sat there for a minute or two, stunned, still in the middle of the road. They then began to argue as to who should get out and have a look in the road and under the car, in case they really had run over anything. Neither of them relished the task, so they decided to get out together and search. When they did - nothing! There was no mark, scratch, den or any indication that the car had been in contact with anything or anybody. The girls made their way to the Trout in a state of mild shock, but they stayed in the pub only long enough to have one drink as they found themselves unable to settle down and relax there.

They would have been even more uneasy had they known that the Trout itself is said to be haunted, not by Rosamund, but by a naval gentleman who appears at the bar in uniform and, having given his order, vanishes without either paying for it or consuming it. As it was, the friends went back to one of their homes where they told her mother what had happened. They were both still unconvinced that they had not been in contact with anything. They were advised to wait and see if any such incident was reported in the local paper, but, despite examining it very carefully, they could learn nothing. The driver avoided that stretch of road and, instead of being sceptical of other people's experiences as she once had been, she confessed to being, 'quite amazed and excited' when she learned of what the party of students had seen on Port Meadow.

A creepy little tale has been passed down concerning a certain vicar of **Wolvercote** who, late one dark night in 1744, was making his way back home from Oxford. All of a sudden, his lantern went out for no apparent reason. As he stood there in the darkness, perplexed and wondering what he should do, he heard a child crying nearby. Then, just as suddenly as it had gone out, his lantern flared back to life again. In its light, he was able to make out a second lantern sitting by the side of the road. The Vicar, realising then that something was expected of him, rushed off to find a spade. He set to work digging at the spot that the lantern indicated, and eventually discovered the skeleton of a child. The kindly man collected up the bones and gave them a Christian burial in his own churchyard. Over the years, a story had evolved relating that the crying child was one which had been accidentally shot by the Royalist guard defending Godstow House during the Civil War. Whatever the child's true identity, he or she certainly seems to have a ready-made ghostly family living in and around Port Meadow.

CHAPTER THREE:
WEST OXFORDSHIRE

Tourist Information Centres:
Burford: *The Brewery, Sheep Street, Burford, OX18 4LP*
Tel: 01993 823558
Chipping Norton: *The Guildhall, Chipping Norton, OX7 5NJ*
Tel: 01608 644379
Witney: *The Town Hall, 51A Market Square, Witney, OX8 6AG*
Tel: 01993 775802
Woodstock: *Hensington Road, Woodstock, OX20 1JQ*
Tel: 01993 811038

Sandwiched in a fan-shaped area between the A40 and the A34, with no main roads crossing the area, West Oxfordshire ghosts are, like its villages and its folklore, a mixture of old and new, traditional and modern, but with a distinct leaning towards the ancient! They include some of the best authenticated, as well as those that are little more than myths.

With Milton and Shipton, **Ascott under Wychwood** is one of three villages with Wychwood in its title. The name is thought to derive from 'Hwicca's wood', and have no connection with witches. Wychwood was originally a royal forest, which, at its fullest extent, stretched from Bladon to Burford, a distance of some twelve miles. Parts of it survive to this day but to nothing like it did before disafforestation in 1857.

The Whit Hunt, which originated in Saxon times, was once a great festival for all the settlements in the forest, each village sending a Morris dancing team which danced from place to place. Unfortunately, the fair which evolved from the hunt degenerated into a drunken affair, detrimental to public morals, a haunt of tricksters and charlatans, travellers and pickpockets, until it was suppressed by the Duke of Marlborough in the mid-nineteenth century.

Ascott lies in the valley of the Evenlode, a grey stone little place clustered round its Norman church. It also boasts a Neolithic long barrow, a section of which has been reconstructed in the County Museum at Woodstock. About fifty skeletons were found in the barrow, buried in a low, stone lined chamber. It has been estimated that most of them had died in their 20's, although the age range was between a few months and fifty years. The average height was 5'5" and several showed signs of a disability similar to spina bifida.

It is not the spirit of a long dead Stone Age Ascott resident or even of one of the revellers at the Whit Hunt which haunts Ascott Grange, however, but a much gentler ghost. It is said locally that in the nineteenth century a maid servant at the Grange threw herself from an upstairs window. Unfortunately, we know nothing more than this about the unfortunate girl, not even her name, only the fact that she used to pick lavender and sell it. Even now, from time to time, a sudden and inexplicable scent of lavender is experienced and, although floorboards have been taken up in attempts to discover the source, nothing has ever been found.

A phantom coach is reputed to career round the village at full tilt, round corners and along roads leading in and out of Ascott. This could well be a former Duke of Marlborough dealing out rough justice to fair revellers, or one of his agents collecting overdue rents or tracking down poachers; whatever the origin of the event, it obviously made such an impression locally that its echoes survive to this day.

Bampton, like its namesake in Devon, was once famous for its horse fair. The name is thought to derive from `Beam', a reference to all the trees which grew in the vicinity, indeed, until the middle of the nineteenth century, no proper roads led to the town.

The parish was unusual in that until the nineteenth century, it had three vicars, each with his own vicarage and churchwarden. The vicarages occupied three sides of the churchyard, with a deanery on the other. Each incumbent took charge for four months and then went off to another parish, the living of which was held by the same patron. The parish registers show the results of these three different versions of local surnames. There is a West Oxfordshire saying, 'to quarrel like the vicars of Bampton.' The stately church of St Mary the Virgin, which has good examples from all the great architectural periods, is on a Saxon site. In the north transept lies a battered fifteenth-century knight, probably a member of the Talbot family whose name lives on in a local inn.

Now only a shadow of its medieval self, Bampton is still very much a centre of old traditions and folklore. Its main claim to fame today is that, along with Headington, it is a leading centre of Morris dancing. One of the pubs has been renamed the Morris Clown in honour of one of the characters, the Clown, or Fool, who bears a sword on which is impaled a plum cake in a tin. A slice of this cake is guaranteed to bring luck to the purchaser.

Other Bampton events are the Pumpkin Club's annual street fair and the Whit Monday Great Shirt race. The Race, they would have one believe, dates back to the year 784 and recalls the time when Ethelred the Shirtless pursued the burghers of Bampton through the streets `in order to obtain a shirt for his back'. What success he met with, and why he was shirtless in the first place, we shall never know, but in reality the race is a nineteenth-century event, revived in 1952. The name comes from the rule that all entrants must wear long garments. It consists of 2-men teams who race from pub to pub - there are about ten in the town - and toss down half a pint in each. Transport takes the form of makeshift vehicles of any kind, one of the favourites being the pram. The winners get an inscribed tankard and a bowl of ale. In addition to providing plenty of entertainment, the Shirt Race raises money for charity.

One house in Bampton had a particularly bad reputation for being haunted. One record from as long ago as 1661 tells of a distressing series of events which happened to a family named Wood. The haunting took the form of loud knocks at the door, which were correctly interpreted as messengers of doom heralding a forthcoming death in the family. On one occasion these were loud enough to cause three great pans of lard to shake and totter on a shelf in the dairy. Within a few months, Captain Wood's wife, mother, and niece had all died. Eventually the Captain abandoned the Bampton house for a more welcoming one at nearby Brize Norton. Two centuries later the house was still known for its eerie and inexplicable scampering noises which went up and down the stairs. These only ceased when a new owner had the roof replaced.

A similar connexion between a roof and a haunting is told of the Talbot inn. A few weeks after moving in, a new landlord and his wife, happily unaware of the existence of Horace the resident ghost, were alone in the bar

Bampton churchyard

when they heard heavy male footsteps. These came from an upstairs corridor, but investigation showed that no one visible was up there. The landlord told this story to a customer who remembered having being told something similar by the previous landlord. A guest, also unaware of Horace, had been so badly disturbed by the sound of someone walking around outside his room that he got out of bed in a temper, determined to tell the wanderer exactly what he thought of him. Again, no one was there.

Suggestions have been made that the ghost is that of a little old man who emerges from a tiny garret under the roof. Furthermore, he could even be the Original Bampton Ghost who was dislodged from the Woods' house when it was reroofed. The attic theory is supported by the fact that during the previous landlord's tenancy, structural alterations were carried out in this part of the Talbot and these included the creation of a new bedroom out of that part of a landing onto which the attic stairs had formerly led.

In 1958, a USAF major from Brize Norton and his wife were occupying the new room when the lady awoke to see a shadowy form emerge from a cupboard. This had been made out of the bottom part of the old attic staircase. This figure flitted across the room and made its way towards the landing. The next morning the lady said that, although she had been unable to make out any features and had heard no sound, she was convinced that what she had seen was a human form. Horace's adventures at the Talbot Hotel have been covered by the *Oxford Times*, 8th and 15th July 1960, and the *Witney Gazette*, 22nd November 1973. Does the Talbot harbour two ghosts, one silent, and one heavy footed, perhaps? Did the fact that Major and Mrs Z came from Brize Norton awaken old memories for the ghost, and make him think that his old victim, Captain Wood, had returned for him to torment?

In addition to Horace, Bampton has an exceptional number of ghosts and mysterious visitors. For instance, there is a lady ghost who has been laid in a barrel of beer and shut up in a cellar at the Manor. She is popularly supposed to be a Mrs Whittaker whose husband fell for the charms of a housemaid. When Mrs Whittaker learned of this she fell into a decline and died of the proverbial broken heart, only to return and haunt the Manor in which she had known such distress while alive. Like many another Oxfordshire ghost, hers was initially laid in a pond which subsequently dried up and so permitted her to escape and haunt again. So far, the second laying in the beer barrel seems successful.

Other hauntings in the Bampton area include a room in a cottage at Manor Farm, Lew, where in 1971 a couple of American families who lived there used to hear a bell ringing for no apparent reason. One wonders if the Bampton ghosts find transatlantic visitors more rewarding than British ones who might be a little more blasé; also if the Lew residents and Major and Mrs Z ever got to hear of each other's experiences.

A rolling object resembling a woolpack travels round the countryside at a cracking pace and then vanishes into a fishpond at Ham Court in yet another example of the involvement of water in hauntings, and assorted animal wraiths patrol local byways.

Last and certainly not least, a naked man has been seen by the wayside for a few seconds only, in true flasher style. The place in which this apparition manifests itself is not told to many, possibly for fear of crowds rushing to the spot in anticipation.

Burford, 'the Gateway to the Cotswolds', lies on a steep hill leading from the A40 some 20 miles west of Oxford. The centre consists of a long main street which slopes steeply down to the river Windrush. This lovely place is lined with boutiques, tea-rooms and specialist shops, courtyards and gabled houses. An outstanding example is the Tolsey, a former customs house which is now Burford Museum and shelters market stalls at ground level. Between the shops and houses run alleyways known locally as tchures. Burford is a centre for local crafts, principally leather and woollen goods, and, of course, tourism. Near the bridge over the Windrush is a row of almshouses dating back to 1457, which were rebuilt in 1828, and the grammar school which was endowed by Symeon Wysdom in 1576.

Burford is rightly proud of its great wool church, a Norman foundation, light and spacious, with an oaken roof and slender spire which can be seen for miles. Its moment of drama came in 1649 when a group of four hundred Levellers, in revolt against Cromwell's administration, were rounded up and herded into the church. It was then used as a temporary gaol and round the lead rim of the font is carved in rough lettering, `Anthony Sedley Prisner 1649'. Three of the prisoners were lined up against the church wall and shot as an example; the bullet marks can be seen to this day. The remainder were packed off to Ireland.

Inside the church can be seen the alabaster tomb of Sir Lawrence Tanfield, Chief Baron of the exchequer in the reign of Queen Elizabeth I, and the builder of Burford Priory. Here he lies with his wife, Sir Lawrence in ruff and scarlet-lined cloak, she dressed in black and gold. Nearby are their daughter Elizabeth, wife of the 1st Viscount Falkland, and also Lucius Cary, Lord Falkland, the Royalist hero who sold the Priory to William Lenthall, Speaker of the House of Commons, who is also buried in this church. In 1620, Sir Lawrence Tanfield issued a writ against some burgesses of the town on the grounds that they had usurped certain manorial privileges. Might triumphed over right and Tanfield's wife seized control of the property after his death. So evil was the impression which she made that she is said to haunt the town by flying over the rooftops in a blazing coach. Another version of the story has Tanfield himself driving a phantom team over the Burford skyline. Such nuisance did the pair become that the people of Burford petitioned a local clergyman to perform an exorcism. At length Lady Tanfield's spirit was trapped in a glass bottle. This was corked up and cast into the Windrush, near the bridge. Should this bottle ever rise up and float, so allowing the cork to dry out, her spirit may be released. For this reason the townspeople used to top up the river with buckets of water at times of drought.

Burford Priory, rebuilt at the beginning of the nineteenth century, has a seventeenth-century chapel. The Priory has been a convent for Anglo-Catholic Benedictine nuns since 1947 and has long had the reputation of being haunted by a small brown monk! In addition, at two in the morning, the monks' old prayer time of prime, a bell sometimes rings out and a choir is heard singing there. A disused room in the Priory harbours a very noisy ghost or poltergeist which throws things around in a violent fashion; in this part of the building an oppressive feeling of sadness is experienced.

Around the grounds of Burford Rectory stalks a phantom gamekeeper, walking through solid objects and carrying a blunderbuss. This may be accounted for by the fact that Speaker Lenthall's servant John Prior was found murdered in this garden, or perhaps one of the three hanged Levellers continues to bear arms.

Along the road leading from Burford to Minster Lovell thunders a mysterious black cloud which is accorded supernatural attributes by local people according to the *Witney Gazette*, 22nd November 1973.

Burford, Tanner monument in church

Twenty miles north west of Oxford is **Chipping Norton**, the highest town in the county. The name means the northern trading place.

'Chippy' has a fine large medieval 'wool' church, reached by a steep lane in which there are some seventeenth-century almshouses, with fine wrought iron railings which support an ornamental stone gateway. St Mary's dates chiefly from the later Middle Ages, incorporating the remains of an older building. According to the *Witney Gazette*, 22nd November 1973, the tower is haunted by the shade of a former vicar who, in 1549, became involved in an uprising against the passing of the First Act of Uniformity, which enforced the use of the First Prayer Book of Edward VI. The protesters were speedily put down by the 1,500 troops called out to deal with them and the ecclesiastical troublemaker was hanged from his own church tower.

Many of the houses in the town centre are made of the local Cotswold stone and in one of them lived Mr T and his two young daughters. One night, when Mr T was in bed, he heard the patter of small feet go along the passage to the bathroom. He thought nothing of this until several minutes had passed and the footsteps did not return. Mr T got out of bed to check. He did not need to switch on the light, as there was a street lamp which lit the passage quite adequately. On a small landing between the first and second floors, a small girl was sitting and at first Mr T thought it was his elder daughter, so alike were they in age and appearance. Mr T asked what was the matter and why she was sitting there. The girl was very blond, with hair which curled up at the ends, and she wore an old-fashioned nightdress with a high, frilled collar. She made no attempt to answer him and Mr T noticed that she was crying. She then got up, still without saying a word, and started to go up the second flight of stairs which led to the girls' bedroom. Mr T followed her and quickly switched on the light. When she reached about halfway up the stairs, the girl vanished. He went on up to the girls' room and found them both sound asleep. Mr T is certain that he was not asleep when he met this sad little girl, as he remembers noticing his unnaturally deep and throaty voice when he spoke to her, because he had a slight cold at the time.

Cornbury Park, just south of Charlbury, had its origins in a royal hunting lodge in Wychwood Forest and is run as a sporting estate today. Among its tenants was Robert Dudley, Earl of Leicester, a favourite of Queen

Elizabeth I. The house is sixteenth-century, with additions and renovations made in 1631, and later alterations were carried out by Lord Chancellor Clarendon, father of James II's queen, Anne Hyde. In the eighteenth century, the house was the venue for secret meetings of Jacobite sympathisers and it is even said that the Young Pretender himself, Charles Edward Stuart, came there in 1750.

The Cornbury ghost is that of Amy Robsart, wife of Robert Dudley. She was found at the bottom of a flight of stairs with her neck broken, at their home in Cumnor Place, near Abingdon. The circumstances of her death were more than a little suspicious and Dudley attracted a good deal of criticism for his treatment of Amy, even before her death. Rumour suggested that her demise was very convenient, for, as Anthony Wood wrote,

"Robert Dudley, earle of Leicester, a man of very goodly person and singularly well-featured, being much in grace and a great favourite with Queen Elizabeth, it was thought and commonly rumor'd that if soe be he had bin but a bachelour or a widdower, the Queen would have made him her husband."

As it was, even the Queen dared not go ahead with such a venture, so hostile was the feeling against it.

After her death, hasty burial and subsequent reburial in the University church of St Mary the Virgin in Oxford, Amy seems to have returned to appear before the startled Dudley while he was staying at Cornbury. Catching him unawares while out hunting, she informed him that within ten days he would be as she then was. At this comforting piece of news, he went back to the house and, just as Amy had predicted, died within the stated time.

In *The Charlbury of Our Childhood, 1845-1860*, Miss CW Pumphrey tells the story as she heard it as a child: "There was once a bad nobleman a-visiting at Cornbury and one night when he'd been out hunting and was along the BroadLight a'most by the Forest Plain, the ghost of his lady as some say he'd murdered came to him and said, 'In ten days you'll be as I be.' An' he went back to Charlbury and in ten days he was dead. An' poor Jim were a-walkin' there and he seed it, so then he knew as his time were come and he went home and took to his bed that very night and he died within the week. An' he be'n't the only one as I've heard of as died that way.'

Dudley's own ghost is also said to walk near Beech Row and Lower Light, so perhaps the couple have been reunited in death at Cornbury Park.

Neat and Church Enstone are about 15 miles from Oxford on the A34, Neat Enstone along the main road, and Church Enstone tucked away down a side road and easily missed by the traffic hurtling along towards the Midlands.

A ghostly experience was reported in the *Oxford Mail* of 14th November 1969. It concerned Mr A, a stockman working on a farm in Chipping Norton. In 1969, he was walking the half mile or so from his home in the hamlet of Fulwell to his regular, the Bell Inn at Neat Enstone, as was his usual practice. His way lay along a lane, above which the trees hung like the vaulting of a church roof. He took his torch with him and was not at all nervous for his job had made him used to the dark and, besides, he knew every inch of his walk. He had just switched his torch off when he became aware of something walking alongside him. Whatever it was seemed to be the figure of a man, all in white and wearing a cap. It stayed silent all the time that it paced along with him. This strange escort accompanied Mr A for about 50 yards and then disappeared. As he put on the torch again, he saw that the Thing was ahead of him along the leafy lane. It seemed to wait until he drew level and then it vanished again. Mr A said that he felt numb all the way up his back, but insisted that he was afraid of no human being and that he was convinced that what he had seen was some kind of apparition. The following night, the landlord of the Bell set out with his guard dog to accompany Mr A from his cottage to the pub, but there was no sign of the figure that night, nor has it been reported since.

The haunting at Church Enstone happened at Pear Tree Cottage, a lovely stone and slate building, with stained glass heraldic crests set into the windows, a suitable home for genealogist, Mr M, who told his story to the *Oxford Mail,* 2nd August 1978. Mr M's troubles started as soon as he moved into the cottage, before his furniture had even arrived. He was using a camp bed and was unable to sleep because of the unnatural cold, so, about three in the morning, he took a hot bath to warm himself up and tried to get to sleep. It was impossible and he spent the night shivering. The same coldness came over him for the next three Sundays, then he went away for the weekend, but on the following Sunday it was even worse, so he put two more blankets on the bed. While still kept awake by the cold, the extra blankets having proved useless, Mr M turned over in bed and caught sight of a sort of luminous disc which vanished as soon as he put the light on. Mr M put on his glasses to get a better look, and, as he watched, the dial slowly took on the shape of what he thought was a cat's face. While he was watching the cat, he became aware of the shape of a cross, very dim at first and then gaining strength, until both cross and cat faded away again. As they did, the room grew gradually warmer. When these sightings appeared again, Mr M called in a couple of his neighbours, one of whom thought that the cat's face was in fact a skull. After they left, Mr M put a thick towel, f olded double, against the place where they had been, but, at midnight, both were clearly visible, shining through the material of the towel. Once more, the room was very cold and Mr M, catching sight of himself in a mirror, noticed that his hair was standing on end.

The following morning found Mr M's dustbin sitting in the kitchen, its contents strewn all round it. It would have had to come through two locked doors to arrive in the kitchen. On going into his study, Mr M saw that his Bible on the bureau had been torn in half and a copy of the Book of Mormon had been ripped into tiny pieces in one corner, while the remains of a Koran lay in the other.

Later, the Vicar of Enstone came to Pear Tree Cottage to see the cross and skull and returned the following morning to exorcise the bedroom and bless the study and the hall. All in vain, for the images returned as usual, this time vanishing with an enormous bang. By this time, Mr M had had enough. He decided to do some investigating and started to scratch and scrape away at the whitewash on the bedroom wall. Soon he came to some flowered wallpaper, then, having ripped this off, some paper which was stuck unto the wall itself. On this was sketched the outline of a very crudely drawn skull, beside which was a cross from which hung an upside down human figure. Mr M managed to obliterate these markings, and from then onwards they did not appear to him again. However, no watch would ever work in the bedroom again, and the alarm clock took to waking him at all hours of the night. Once again the Vicar came and suggested that an expert on exorcism be consulted. This gentleman advised a full exorcism be performed, which Mr M readily agreed to. Holy Communion was celebrated in the study and the Vicar marked every windowpane and mirror in the cottage with a sign of the cross. These were supposed to be left untouched, but the cleaning lady inadvertently wiped them off the study mirror and ever since Mr M's watches again have refused to work properly in the bedroom.

The small market town of **Eynsham** (pronounced `Enshum') lies 7 miles north west of Oxford, off the A40. The area has been settled since at least the sixth century AD, as shown by the group of twenty sunken huts discovered at New Wintles farm. The first written reference to Eynsham appears in the Anglo-Saxon Chronicle for 571, then little is known until the foundation of the Benedictine Abbey in 1005. This stood in the meadows near where the parish church is today, and some of the stained glass taken from the abbey after the Dissolution of the Monasteries has found its way into the church. Acre End, better known as the setting for a book by the late Mollie Harris, Martha Woodford in The Archers, appears to have been the original nucleus of the town, but later this moved to outside the abbey gates, creating the present Market Place.

In the main thoroughfare stands the Railway Inn, whose landlord, Paul Littlechild, was forced to leave the pub in 1967 because of the disturbances there. He had been told that, for a century at least, the cellar had been haunted by the victim of a murder which had been committed there. As he told the *Sunday Mirror,* of 2nd April 1967, among the strange happenings were the time that the beer stopped flowing because the pressure had suddenly turned off of its own accord, the way that the fridge would stop working every so often, and the rattling of the cellar doors during the night when no one was around. Eventually Mr Littlechild had enough of the noises that he had heard over the years which he had spent in the Railway Inn and he started to remain upstairs whenever he heard them, rather than go to investigate as he had done previously. The ghost obviously had far stronger nerves than those of its unfortunate human victim; Mr Littlechild freely admitted to being `scared out of his wits.'His experiences were covered also by *Witney Gazette*, of 22nd November 1973.

Between Witney and Eynsham the A 40 now crosses what is said to be an ancient monkish burial ground, and the fact that there was a notorious accident black spot there was blamed on the fact that the long dead monks were registering their disapproval of this abuse of consecrated ground. In 1970, Mr and Mrs W were returning to Eynsham in their car after spending a convivial evening with friends in Witney. As they sped along the A40, their minds were more on the pleasant time they had just spent, and far from the supernatural. Suddenly, as they were passing the turn off to Barnard Gate, a pale human form flitted quite casually across the road, right in the path of their car, causing Mr W to brake violently. The couple turned to each other open mouthed, but it was quite unnecessary for them to ask each other if they had seen the stroller. Neither Mr nor Mrs W had ever heard about the burial ground or the frequent accidents for which this stretch of the A 40 was notorious.

Near the Oxfordshire-Gloucestershire border, **Kingham** has a 17th-century Grange and Rectory, and a neat little 14th-century church with unusual pews made of carved stone with wooden seats.

The Langstone Arms hotel, scene of the Kingham haunting, is a 19th-century building. Its good-natured ghost first made its presence heard, seen and felt in the early 1960's. An expert on exorcism who was called in to deal with it declined to do so, as he felt that it was friendly and should therefore be left well alone. According to his initial way of thinking, it is a mistake to attempt to exorcise a friendly spirit, although he may have revised his opinion when one showed its feelings by tipping him out of bed.

By 1964, the apparition was revealing itself to the hotel staff on a regular basis. It would come every ten days, its arrival being heralded by a noise similar to coughing, followed by shuffling footsteps. Then the ghost would actually appear, a white female shape, about 5'3" in height and wearing some sort of head dress. She would then glide along the hotel corridors, Room Number One being her chosen venue. It was noted that dogs were particularly upset in this room. All the staff of the Langstone Arms, together with several regular customers, admitted to having seen her and the manager stated that she had, 'put the wind up almost everybody.' Mr S himself had been a non-believer in the supernatural until the ghost arrived to convert him. The Vicar of Kingham, too, was somewhat sceptical until he was told about her by several different people. The Vicar, Rev Attwood-Evans, conducted some research into the history of the hotel, but found nothing, like a murder or suicide, to furnish a clue as to the visitor's identity. She might have been connected in some way with an earlier building on the site, but until more evidence is found, she will have to remain just another White Lady.

Sometimes pronounced 'Nor Lye' locally, **North Leigh** is a rapidly expanding village fast becoming a dormitory for Witney and Oxford. It has a ruined windmill and assortment of building styles which includes stone and thatched cottages, modern bungalows, and council houses. It has a church to be proud of, Saxon in origin and containing much Norman work. Its main attraction is the Wilcote chapel which contains a splendid fifteenth-century alabaster tomb of a member of the Wilcote family. An imposing Doom painting shows scenes of the Last Judgement, with the dead rising from their coffins, angels, and the burning pit. Older than anything in the church, however, are the remains of a Roman villa which was discovered in the nineteenth century in the hamlet of East End and once consisted of some sixty rooms arranged around three sides of a courtyard.

Unfortunately, less is known about the age or history of the two ghostly ladies who frequent North Leigh; all that is told of them is that one is black, the other white, and that one haunts an orchard while the other, like so many others, prefers a pond.

To the north east of Chipping Norton is its attractive hamlet-suburb of **Over Norton**. With creeper covered houses, this would seem the perfect setting for a good old fashioned haunting, but the house in question is a council house, then only about thirty years old.

In 1965, the B family, consisting of Mr and Mrs B and their three children, was disturbed by a series of strange and inexplicable happenings. As they told the *Birmingham Post*, 7th May 1965, the action was centred on the staircase and the trapdoor above it which gave access to the loft.

This trapdoor was found open several times a day and on one occasion a nearby light bulb and shade were taken down and placed in the hall. In addition, the front door was found locked, and the key missing.

One day, the youngest child, then aged about one year, was spotted looking up the stairs and laughing at an invisible someone who stood there. These happenings would take place in the daytime only, but then, one evening, while a babysitter was alone in the house, someone, or something, locked the front door from the inside. Then, a few days later, Mrs B heard a sound similar to that of a glass bell being tapped. On investigating, she found that the landing light shade had been put on the stairs, and the bulb from it was sitting on the telephone table near the front door. Later the same day, she tried to get back in through the front door after having been out in the garden, only to discover that she had been locked out. She managed to get back in with the help of a neighbour, and found that the front door key was missing from the lock. It turned up lying in the loft, where Mr B found it as he was closing the trapdoor yet again. The day after that, flowers were removed from a vase in the sitting room and scattered around upstairs. The previous tenants of the Over Norton council house, who had occupied it for seven years, also reported strange happenings there.

Not far from Ascott under Wychwood is **Pudlicote**, a hamlet with a great house and very little else apart from its ghost and the memory of an infamous resident of the hamlet.

The ghost makes it appearance at the crossroads formed by the junction of the A 361 road to Chipping Norton and the side road leading to Pudlicote House. It is a figure in white which flits out from behind the bushes, crosses the main road terrifying any locals or motorists who happen to be passing, and then makes its way towards a quarry where it vanishes. The figure was particularly active in the 1960's when it was reported on several occasions. Locally, the ghost is said to be that of an old character by the name of 'Gran' who seems to have been some sort of squatter who lived rough in the vicinity of the crossroads. 'Gran' is reputed to have amassed a small fortune in gold guineas which she kept in her cramped lodgings, and it is thought that she guards it still, patrolling the cross roads on cold, windy, winter's nights.

The hamlet's criminal is a member of the local gentry, who, while not exactly a ghost as such, ended up as a terrible example to those with similar thieving tendencies to those he possessed himself. This de Pudlicote, at a time when he was undergoing a cash flow problem, heard about the Chamber of the Pyx at Westminster, probably from one of the monks of Eynsham Abbey. This chamber, he was told, was used as a bank vault by royalty, who stored in it gold and silver coins, plate, jewellery and every other conceivable sort of treasure. De Pudlicote soon assembled a little band of willing helpers, waited until the king, Edward the First, went off to hammer the Scots north of the Border, and then went up to London to 'case the joint'. They found that it would not be possible for them to force the door of the Chamber of the Pyx, so they decided to make a hole through the wall instead. They had to work by night, slowly and carefully, for there was a dormitory of monks snoring away above the Chamber. By chance, some of these monks came from Eynsham. For four long months this nocturnal labouring continued, gradually progressing along a passage which they dug into the massive walls. They had, at each step, to clear up after themselves before daybreak so that their work would not be detected.

At last they broke through and the jubilant de Pudlicote crept into the Chamber and started to hand the loot out to his gang. Alas, his joy was short lived and so was de Pudlicote himself. The inevitable happened and they were caught red handed. The monks, including those from Eynsham, were sent to the Tower of London, as a punishment for involving themselves in the plot, or at least turning a deaf ear, for they must have known what was going on under their very beds. They were released, however, after two years, for lack of evidence. De Pudlicote's accomplices did not escape so lightly. They were hanged, but his own fate was far worse. He was skinned, and his hide nailed to the door of the Chamber as a horrible warning to those with similar ideas. It can be seen there to this day, black and leathery after six centuries and enough to make any spirit restless.

Spelsbury, with its rows of thatched cottages, would not disgrace any book on beautiful Britain. It follows the road from Charlbury to Chipping Norton in an attractively sinuous way, and a lane leads down from the main road to the church, vicarage and a farmhouse.

A local ghost has been recorded in the hamlet of Taston, according to Elsie Corbett's book, Spelsbury, which was published in 1962. The name derives from Thor's Stone, a lone monolith which is still there today. It is popularly supposed to have been used for pagan worship and acquired such an evil reputation over the centuries that a cross was erected nearby in an attempt to sap its influence.

The ghost which appeared at Taston in the 1830's, however, was no primitive, unknown force, quite the opposite for it was easily recognisable by both the parties to whom it manifested itself. Mr Harris of Middle Farm was courting the Widow Claridge of Lower Farm. They were talking by the door one evening when the ghost of the late Mr Claridge brushed past between them and continued into the house. Mr Harris was so upset by this pointed intrusion that he called off the forthcoming wedding.

Richard Claridge had dropped dead at the age of 45, and was buried on 9th September 1836. On his grave was inscribed:

> A sudden call, I in a moment fell,
> I had no time to bid my friends farewell,
> So you, my neighbours, a warning take,
> And love my children for my sake.

The loving was obviously not supposed to extend to Richard Claridge's widow!

Another Spelsbury haunting which Elsie Corbett describes concerns a Mr Webb, a baker at the nearby village of Chadlington. One day, when Mr Corbett was a small boy, Mr Webb came to Manor Farm in a very disturbed state, and asked if he could sit down for a while as he had had a frightening experience. He went on to tell them how he had been driving his bread van from Chadlington into Spelsbury in the dusk when, just as he got to Bob's Corner, he met an old fashioned coach-and-four. It was impossible for him to stop in time and so he drove straight through it! There is a story told locally about a coach-and-four which overturned and was buried in a bog at the bottom of the hill, but another version claims that the vehicle concerned was a wagon and horses.

Spelsbury is fortunate in having one of the many White Ladies to be found in the Oxfordshire countryside. This one appears in the lane leading from the main road to the church. There are several accounts of her activities on different occasions, but they all agree that a semi-transparent lady can be distinguished in a field south of the church where two footpaths meet. Her journey starts from the crossroads, and ends at a certain ditch where she disappears.

Stanton Harcourt lies off the B449, about 8 miles west of Oxford. It is a village of thatched cottages and an ancient church which is of Norman origin, and contains monuments to the Harcourt family, including that of Robert Harcourt, standard bearer to Henry VII in 1485 at Bosworth Field. Above the tomb are a plumed helmet and a fragment of the flag which he carried at the battle. Not much survives of the old house of the Harcourts, their seat until they moved to Nuneham Courtenay in the eighteenth century. The house at Stanton fell into ruin and was largely demolished in 1789. All that remains is a tower, some fishponds, a sixteenth-century gatehouse and a kitchen with large ovens and an enormous fireplace. The tower is known as Pope's Tower because it was there that he translated Homer's Illiad into English and scratched on a pane of glass, "In the year 1718 Alexander Pope finished here the fifth volume of Homer."
Not surprisingly, this collection of ancient buildings is said to be haunted. The ghost is that of Lady Alice Harcourt who was murdered in the tower at some time in the Middle Ages. One morning, while the rest of the household was at Mass, the murderers crept up the tower steps and hacked

her to pieces. They then tossed the remains out of the window. In some versions of the story, it is the family chaplain who is the murderer. Alice's shade, reassembled once again, used to haunt the grounds until she was laid in one of the fishponds in yet another liquid exorcism. Pope mentions Lady Alice's ghost in a letter to a friends, and the guide book to Stanton Harcourt Manor lists her fishpond as one of its attractions.

A second Stanton Harcourt spirit is Mrs Hall who was in the habit of haunting not only Manor Farm, but also the Harcourt Arms. Mrs Hall poisoned herself after discovering that her husband was associating with the pub landlady. This ghost too was laid in a nearby pond and like Lady Alice is expected to reappear if ever it dries up. The parish registers show two burials for persons named Hall, Elizabeth, on 25th October, 1789 (there is no mention of suicide), and John on 20th January, 1799; they were aged 55 and 66 respectively. It seems that Mrs Hall killed herself the year that the house was demolished, but that John survived another ten years to enjoy the favours of the landlady.

The village of **Stonesfield** occupies a rather bleak position on a small hill and has winding streets which spiral around. The older-style buildings are in the local stone, grey sandstone which can be found in Oxford colleges. Until recently, the slate working for which the village is famous was its chief occupation, virtually the only one apart from agriculture. Recently Stonesfield has become a desirable dormitory for Oxford and Witney workers and much new construction has taken place.

All around the village spreads a vast graveyard of prehistoric creatures whose fossilised skeletons have been unearthed here by the dozen.

Outside the church of St James stands a stone lock up, an iron grille set into its studded oak door, a grim sort of place which acted as an early prison for the unruly of Stonesfield. The church itself is light and airy, if somewhat squat, with white walls, and some interesting old glass showing heraldic shields and black and gold roundels.

A lady who lived in the village, Mrs T, had several experiences of a distressing nature, one of the reasons why they sold a house which had been in the family for generations. One day they were in bed in the front bedroom when Mrs T suddenly noticed a short white figure by the side of the bed. She was, in her own words, 'frightened to bits.' She nudged her husband who woke up but did not see the figure. The following night, on the other side of the bed, Mrs T saw another figure, also white, but taller than the first one.

The next apparition was seen by S, the couple's elder daughter, in the other front bedroom. She saw a man wearing a hat walk straight through a wall. S was too frightened to talk about it at the time, but later told her parents what she had seen.

Mr T announced one day to a relative that he too had seen a man with a dark suit who also passed through a wall in the bedroom. Mrs T was astonished to hear this, as her husband had never mentioned it in front of her before.

One day Mrs T was in the kitchen, and was wearing an overall, in the pocket of which was a bag of Revels sweets. She had been dipping into the bag while doing her housework. Suddenly, something told her to look inside the sweet bag in her pocket. To her amazement, she saw an earring glinting away among the sweets. She immediately pulled it out, and saw that it was an expensive one which she only wore when going somewhere special and which spent the rest of the time put safely away on her dressing table. At the time, she was wearing no earrings at all. She rushed upstairs to the drawer where she remembered she had last put the earrings, and there, just as she expected, was its twin.

One Witney Feast day Mrs T was alone in the house while the others were away at the fair, when she distinctly heard someone coming up the gravel drive towards the front door. She waited in vain for the knock which never came. Neither did she hear any footsteps crunching their way back along the gravel. Later, a neighbour had a very similar experience, and looked out of the front bedroom window. No one.

Strange bangs and other sounds have been heard in the house frequently. The loudest was a sort of explosion which came from the kitchen. When the T's plucked up enough courage to take a look, there was nothing at all out of place and no one to be seen. Another unsettling sight was the coal moving around in its scuttle.

The house is not an old one by West Oxfordshire standards. It was built by a neighbour's father and Mr T heard that his wife 'went a little strange there.' Was this caused by the strange goings on, or are they the result of the unfortunate woman's unstable mind?

Tucked away between Finstock and North Leigh, on elevated ground overlooking the Evenlode valley, the tiny hamlet of **Wilcote** is easily missed. It consists of a few up-market cottages, the renovated Elizabethan Wilcote House standing in its own park, the church and Wilcote Grange. According to a local directory, in 1851, the entire population was "9 souls"; presumably this meant ones still attached to bodies. The lonely little church has a Norman doorway, the rest of the fabric being mainly fourteenth-century, and there are a few bramble-covered Victorian graves to one side of the churchyard. The rest is laid to grass.

In February 1984, a lady who used to live at North Leigh and whose father was the local policeman, relates how he had a disturbing time while on point duty at Wilcote at midnight. Strangely enough, with so few mortal residents, he had another policeman for company, and both men gave the same account of what had happened, although neither was very forthcoming about it. All that they would say was they had heard what sounded like a coach and horses travelling at some speed, but had been unable to see anything at all. Wilcote is said to harbour "summat strange" as they put it in those parts, so perhaps one day somebody will admit to having seen whatever it is, although, in such an isolated spot, it seems very unlikely.

Witney, the chief town of West Oxfordshire, is about 11 miles from Oxford along the A40. It is not a tourist centre in the same way that Burford is, but continues to provide an important focal point for the surrounding villages as it has for centuries.

Despite the rapid growth of housing estates, the real Witney remains, with its inviting little 'tchures' or alleyways, flanked by stone walls, and overhung with greenery. The stroller can disappear between wisteria covered cottages and find himself in a winding lane, passing some very desirable little homes, often medieval behind Georgian or Stuart frontages. Covered with creepers and sporting polished doorknockers and fresh paintwork these houses have state-of-the-art interiors. This Witney is found principally at the end of the High Street, past the shops and up a gentle tree-lined slope. Here is the Town Hall, all arches and stone pillars, and the seventeenth-century Butter Cross. The fine broad Church Green is bordered by stone houses, inns, and hotels, and at the far end is the splendid thirteenth-century church of St Mary the Virgin, with almshouses sheltering against the churchyard wall.

For such a venerable place Witney is singularly ghost free, or perhaps the residents do not wish to be associated with "all that rubbish", as one called the supernatural. However, in August 1979, a Mr E was squatting in a disused non-conformist meeting house, whose name and location he stated, but, as it has been converted into a very attractive private house, it is only fair to withhold details. One night, during Mr E's occupation, there was a violent thunderstorm, complete with fork lightening. The burial ground lay to the rear of the building and one of the grave stones was struck by lightening, making the stone to crack just where the name of the deceased was carved, so making it impossible to read the inscription. Mr E wrote in February 1984, "The following day being overclouded, on returning from the shops and entering the house, I saw what I thought was an elderly woman standing in the bathroom, next to the leaking gaspipe. I went into the kitchen-cum-bedroom and made two cups of tea, one for myself and the other for the elderly woman. On asking the woman if she would like a cup of tea, I received no answer, so I put out my hand to shake her hand in a welcoming gesture. My hand went straight through her, and then I realised that this was a ghost, dropping the cup of tea from my hand through the panic and fright that then overtook me. I left the house and stood outside the bathroom window. The fact of the fork lightening smashing the gravestone seemed to suggest to me that the ghost had risen out of that grave, so I killed the panic and fright inside of myself and said a prayer asking the ghost to accept Jesus and return to the grave where Our Lord was waiting to show the way to heaven. The ghost responded by walking along the gravelled path to the graveyard. I could not see the ghost but I saw and heard the gravel moving with every footstep. At the grave, the flower beaker toppled over, and the grass on top of the grave turned yellow and withered. I understood this to be the returning of the ghost to its resting-place."

Eight miles north of Oxford is **Woodstock**, a stylish country town, well known to the tourists who come there from all over the world, both to visit Blenheim Palace and en route for Stratford on Avon. It was one of the last centres of the once thriving Oxfordshire glove-making industry, particularly widespread in the area around Wychwood Forest, thanks to the availability of leather and doeskin. Presentation pairs of Woodstock gloves have been given to such diverse visitors to the town as Queen Elizabeth I and Princess Diana. The town's stone buildings, its stately little 18th-century town hall, its antique shops and boutiques, and its inns like the Bear and the Marlborough Arms combine to give Woodstock an atmosphere of age and prosperity. Opposite the Bear, with ancient stocks outside it, stands the creeper-covered Fletcher's House, home of the Oxfordshire County Museum. On permanent display there is an exhibition showing life in the county from prehistoric times to our own.

The Museum's manager, Mr John Coles, a man well used to having the weight of history bearing down upon him, had an unnerving experience in Fletcher's House in 1979. He described it as similar to being 'dumped in a bath of icy water, and although I was not really scared, my hair stood on end. It took half an hour to brush it back down,' as he said in a press interview. Mr Coles had been alone on duty one autumn afternoon and was in the office at the top of the building away from that part which is open to the public. Then he heard the footsteps. He left the office to investigate, but found no one about. Then the footsteps started up again. This time Mr Coles bided his time and listened as they kept on coming, onwards and upwards, up a wooden staircase towards him, and then . . . right through him! There was still nothing and nobody to be seen. He then tried to reason with the maker of the footsteps, but the only response that he met with was a, 'chilling sensation.' After hearing the Manager's account, two other members of the museum staff admitted to having had what they termed ghostly experiences. Although no stories have come to light to explain the footsteps, John Coles said he was convinced that the County Museum harboured a ghostly resident.

The best known building in Woodstock is Blenheim Palace, seat of the Dukes of Marlborough, and the birthplace of Sir Winston Churchill in 1874. The room in which he was born, and the brass bed itself, are on view to the public. The Palace came into being after the first Duke, John Churchill, was granted the manor or Woodstock by a 'grateful nation' after his victories over the French during the War of the Spanish Succession. The Palace was started in 1705, and took its name from the Battle of Blenheim which Marlborough won in that year. The architect was Vanburgh, and in Blenheim's case he merited the epitaph:
> 'Lie heavy on him earth, for he
> Laid many a heavy weight on thee.'

Covering three acres, the Palace has hundreds of small chimneys, all of them hidden from view. Not surprisingly, partly on account of its sheer size,

Woodstock, site of manor house in Blenheim Park

and partly because of wrangling which went on over its design, the Palace was till unfinished when the Duke died in 1722. When Sarah, his duchess, quarrelled with Queen Anne, the money supply came to an end, so that the reward turned into a white elephant.

The original manor house of Woodstock stood near the north end of the bridge, over the lake in what is now Blenheim Park. The house lasted, in a ruinous condition, until the 18th century, indeed there was enough of it standing for Vanburgh to lodge there during the construction of the Palace. Against the architect's suggestion that the ruins be landscaped artistically, the duchess insisted that they be completely demolished.

The manor had started life as a hunting lodge in Wychwood Forest and was in existence by the 11th century. The Black Prince, who was born there, has a pub named after him in Old Woodstock, to the north of the main town. Henry I had a menagerie and a deer park in the grounds, and in the 12th century Henry II installed his mistress, Rosamund Clifford there. Legend says that she lived in a secret bower, approached by a maze, and Fair Rosamund's Well can still be seen.

One story relates how Henry's queen, Eleanor of Aquitaine, found out about her husband's lady love and traced Rosamund's bower by means of a silken thread which led her to her rival. The thread was planted on a page who attended Rosamund and the queen confronted Henry's mistress in a fit of jealous rage, offering her a choice of dying by poison or by being knifed to death. Another version has it that Rosamund repented of her ways, and yet another that she was eventually discarded by the king. In any case, it is known that she retired to Godstow Nunnery, where she was buried in 1177. In the 16th century, Michael Drayton wrote a poem on the royal love affair, as did Tennyson in Victorian times.

Modern reports indicate that the Fair One walks at Oxford, in the vicinity of the nunnery. Apart from patrolling Port Meadow, she also visits the Palace. Here is an account written by a lady who used to work in the restaurant there and believes that it might well be Rosamund whom she encountered one day in the late 1970's.

'The apparition I saw, it was quite four years ago, was in the shape of a lovely young lady with fair hair, in a cream long dress. The face was very serene and it seemed to have a kind of transparent look.

I was on my own and had gone down from the kitchen to the room where the stores were kept; the fridges were also there. I had to get some ham and tomatoes to make into sandwiches for the counter. When I entered

Woodstock, Blenheim Palace

77

the storeroom I opened the fridge and then looked at the shelf on the side of the room, where we kept the tomatoes. I felt someone was watching me, so that made me look round again: the lady was stood there. So I said, 'What are you doing here, this is out of bounds for anyone except staff?' I closed the fridge door and was about to ask again, 'Who are you?' and it had gone. I then went back to the kitchen and asked if anyone had been there, and they said, 'No, why?' I told them about seeing this lady. We had a very old lady who lived in Woodstock working at the time, and she said, 'G, you have seen Fair Rosamund.' She believed me, but I don't think the other people did. She also told me that she knew of someone else who had seen her. This was, I would think, about 12 midday, in June or July. In fact I dismissed it because no-one apart from the old lady wanted to believe it, but even now, when I think about it, I still see her as she looked."

A ghost seems to have moved into the Palace from the Manor, for it has been seen on several occasions. A young lady staying there reported seeing 'light from the fireplace' in her room, and by the light a man crouched by the fire. The theory is that this may be a Roundhead soldier and if this is the case, it is amusing to recall that in Scott's novel Woodstock, some residents of the old manor, who had Royalist sympathies, pretended to be ghosts and arranged hauntings in order to drive away unwelcome Roundhead guests.

CHAPTER FOUR:
CHERWELL

Tourist Information Centres:
Banbury: *Spiceball Park Road, OX16 2PQ*
Tel: 01295 259855
Bicester: *Unit 6a, Bicester Village, Pingle Drive, Bicester, OX6 7WD*
Tel: 01869 369055

As elsewhere, the ghosts of the Cherwell District come in many guises, from the fully documented to the vaguely outlined. Among the latter type is one found at **Cottisford**, the parish which includes Flora Thompson's hamlet of Juniper Hill, which she calls Larkrise in her book *Larkrise to Candleford*. There, so one may be told, Richard Eyre's spirit was contained not only in a cask, but also in a pond in an attempt to keep its unwelcome presence away from the villagers. At nearby **Fringford**, Rose Brennan, a former landlady, is thought to haunt the Butcher's Arms.

Another example of ghosts passing into folk history is that of the brutal Judge Page who is buried in the church of St Peter and St Paul at **Steeple Aston**, 15 miles north of Oxford. One of the infamous 'hanging' judges, Page commissioned a splendid monument to himself and his wife from the fashionable sculptor Scheemacker. This monument can still be seen to this day in the Lady Chapel at Steeple Aston, but, fine as it seems, Page was quick to spot the sculptor's error in forgetting to carve a wedding ring on Lady Page's hand and, after considerable wrangling, deducted £20 from his fee. Local legend relates how, at midnight, the widows of the hundred men whom Page condemned to be hanged, turn into owls and chase him in a beer barrel up and down Middle Aston pond.

Other strange happenings seem to have been one-offs. According to the *Oxford Journal*, 31st August 1979, at **Charlton on Otmoor**, in 1979, Nickie Davis awoke in the night to find a woman dressed in black holding a lantern. Then, a few weeks later, she saw an elderly man in a white smock. Later Nickie discovered that an 18-year-old girl called Rosalind had died from blood poisoning when she miscarried an illegitimate child fathered by her teenaged boyfriend. Local people tell how Rosalind died in what was to become Nickie's bedroom, and conclude that the elderly couple were her distraught parents, vainly trying to save her life.

At **Fencott**, deep in the wilds of Otmoor, an Army corporal and his wife moved into five-bedroomed Manor Farmhouse in 1959. Their pleasure at having their own house was soon spoiled by doors inexplicably opening and shutting in the night, tapping sounds on the walls of different rooms, and by their dog growling at an invisible 'something.' (*Oxford Times*, 6th February 1959) The Army authorities investigated, but to no avail. Still on a military theme, the *Oxford Mail*, of 16th September 1961, reported that there was a haunted Nissan hut at Arncott, near Bicester.

At the beginning of the 19th century, the Rector of **Launton**, near Bicester, was a Doctor William Browne, who haunted the rectory there until part of it was demolished. He was said to frequent the corridor above Bishop Skinner's study and was frequently heard there by Mr James Marriott who worked at the rectory as a boy. He has also been heard walking around in other parts of the house by the Reverend CP Sherwood, the Rector who lived there between 1958 and 1962. Dr Browne was in the habit of fining poachers at Bicester Court without bothering to hear the evidence, and villagers say this heartlessness is what made him walk in the afterlife.

On dark winter nights, the lonely country road between **Piddington and Ludgershall**, on the county boundary with Buckinghamshire, is frequented by Gentleman John, a watchmaker from Ludgershall who was murdered on his way home from Piddington in the middle of the 18th century. He was called Gentleman John because of his elegant appearance, and was killed for a gold watch which he was returning to its owner after repairing it. It is doubtful if the murderer was ever caught.

The Reverend Maurice Frost, Vicar of **Deddington**, in the north of the county, about 17 miles north of Oxford died on Christmas Day 1961. However, as was reported in the *Oxford Mail*, 27th April 1962, he continued to wind up his clocks for some time afterwards. The Vicar's cousin, a Mr Jarrett, who had come from Italy to settle his affairs, had a winding handle taken out of his hand, and experienced an assortment of strange happenings. These included beds which were found dented in the morning as if they had been occupied when no-one had touched them, coughs coming from the empty drawing room, and noises in the study. The domestic staff refused to stay on in the house. In time, the clocks were taken from the vicarage and Mr Jarrett said that he hoped that the ghost had gone with them. The staff, however, remained unconvinced and refused to return to the house.

Of Saxon origin, **Banbury** is the only town on the River Cherwell between its source and Oxford, 23 miles to the south.

The A423 between Banbury and Oxford is haunted by a smashed-up red sports car. Sue Ede, a newspaper reporter from Banbury, was driving along when she spotted the car in the middle of the road. She was forced to slam on her brakes to avoid going straight into it, and only narrowly escaped being hit by the car behind. When she stopped, she found to her surprise and disbelief that the red car had completely vanished. Sue looked all around, but there was no trace of it, and so she got back into her own car and, badly shaken, drove off. After she had gone about two miles, what did she see but the same crashed sports car, again in the middle of the road! She stopped, beginning to wonder if there was something wrong with her. She literally rubbed her eyes and took another look. There it was and then, just as before, it disappeared from her sight. This happened one night in 1978 and Sue immediately tried to find out something of what she had by then realised was a phantom vehicle. She mentioned her experience to a colleague at work and he told her that he had heard a rumour about a crashed car which was sometimes seen on that road. He had also heard that that it is supposed to have been driven by an American serviceman who was involved in a smash up several years previously and had lost his life in the accident.

A more traditional ghost haunts the A423 between Deddington and Adderbury. A man on horseback gallops through a gate and onto the road. He pulls the horse straight across the path of oncoming traffic and then vanishes.

At one time Banbury was famous for its cheeses which Shakespeare refers to in *The Merry Wives of Windsor,* and is still noted for its Banbury cakes which are relatives of the Eccles and Chorley kind. The town is best known, however, for its Cross. The nursery rhyme, *Ride a cock horse to Banbury Cross,* is first found in print in the 18th century, although it must have been popular well before then. The 'fine lady' referred to, might be the ubiquitous Queen Elizabeth the First who spent a considerable amount of time in the Oxford area. The cross in the rhyme would have been a medieval one, probably similar to the Eleanor crosses like the one at Charing Cross. At the end of the sixteenth century, Puritan elements among the citizenry engineered its destruction. The present monument, which bears no resemblance to a cross, was erected in 1859 to commemorate the marriage of the Princess Royal to Frederick of Prussia. Even at this late date, descendants of those Puritans were complaining about its 'imagery'. The statues of Queen Victoria, Edward VII, and George V, were added in 1914.

Over the years Banbury acquired a deserved reputation for vandalism. In the seventeenth century the town petitioned Parliament for permission to demolish the castle and, when this was agreed, used the stones for building and repair works in the town. Then, in 1792, the townspeople blew up their ancient church with gunpowder in order to save the expense of repairing it, and gave the excuse that the building was unsafe. Finally, Banbury sold its town plate to Lord North of Wroxton Abbey, although two maces, one from the Commonwealth period, the other Georgian, were brought back home after a convivial lunch at Wroxton.

A reputedly haunted Banbury building is the Town Hall and its adjoining buildings, two workshops and some ancillary rooms. The ghost does not stick to any particular time or season for its hauntings, seeming to prefer the most awkward and embarrassing moments. The Town Hall buildings, which date from at least the middle of the nineteenth century, incorporate parts of an old tavern and once housed the cells of the police station. People who live and work locally believe that the ghost may have some connection with a prisoner who died in the cells, but continues to walk around the building.

In April 1957, Mr BLR, who had a typewriter business in one of the buildings, told an *Oxford Mail* reporter about his experiences there, particularly at weekends, and after shop hours when he had been alone on the premises. Once, he said, he had locked the front door as no one else would be coming in, when he heard distinct footsteps on the narrow stairs. They came along to his workshop door, and then stopped completely and were no more to be heard. Mr R went out to investigate, but found nothing and no one about. He then went out to make sure that there was no one anywhere else round, putting on a brave face when, in fact, he was very scared indeed.

Two years previously, in 1955, he had had a similar experience and was therefore almost sure that he would find nothing. On the first occasion, armed with a torch, he had made a thorough search of the premises and even went up to the top floor where there were some unused rooms, as he had heard someone walking about up there, but could find nothing. Even during the day, added Mr R, customers would come into his shop and, while he was serving them, would ask who was at the door and wonder why he paid no attention to them. When he told them that there was no one there, they would give him strange looks as if to imply that they were certain they had not imagined the noises.

The market town of **Bicester** (pronounced Bister) lies 17½ miles north east of Oxford, on the A421. Bicester reached the peak of its prosperity in the 16th and 17th centuries when much building work was carried out there. Some half-timbered buildings are to be found around Market End, survivors of a series of fires which swept through the town in the early part of the 18th century.

Bicester then experienced a decline in its fortunes for the next century, due largely to the prevalent agricultural depression widespread throughout Oxfordshire and other predominantly rural counties. A new epoch began in the area with the arrival of the RAF station on the outskirts of the town in 1917, and of a large Ordnance depot which provided work for local people. Bicester's population doubled between 1961 and 1971 and advertisements for new houses give the impression that it continues to increase on an almost daily basis.

In his book, *Bicester Wuz a Little Town,* written in 1968, a local author, Sid Hedges, relates a couple of ghost stories. The first concerns the district known as Crockwell. The original Crock Well used to be situated 'in a small enclosure between the roadway and an angle of the high wall forming the boundary of Bicester House gardens.' The well was later covered over by a large stone slab, and a pump installed in its place.

In 1920, a courting couple were making their way towards the girl's home, coming from Field Street, across the Fields, and on into King's End. As they passed the old well, each gave a sudden visible start, but neither said anything, merely increasing the speed at which they were walking.

When they were safely past the well, they began to talk, asking each other to describe what they had just seen. The response was identical. A cloaked figure, dark and rather menacing, similar to the one in the advertisement for Sandeman's port, as they later put it. After a hurried consultation, they plucked up courage to go back and take another look, but saw nothing further to report. Several accounts of this apparition have been heard around the town, but whether they are authentic cannot be proved, as they seem to have taken place after the news spread about the original sighting. A rumour was also current to the effect that the figure had been that some sort of foreigner, probably a Spaniard who 'once upon a time' had been crossed in love by a Bicester girl. This was probably suggested by the appearance of the ghost as described, rather than being founded on any real romantic incident.

A second Bicester haunting, again with watery associations, goes back centuries. It centres on Rookery Pond, or did so until the pond was replaced by the fire station. The ghost is that of a Royalist lady from Bicester House, which was attacked by Parliamentarian forces while its menfolk were away fighting elsewhere. The Roundheads searched high and low for the lady's money and jewels, but in vain, for she had had the foresight to hide them away in Rookery Pond. Her quick thinking, however, was to cost her her life, for the enemy soldiers killed her in their frustration at finding nothing of value. At the time of year when the murder took place, she was said to ride mournfully on horseback round the pond, searching for her hidden hoard, so earning herself the title of the White Lady of Rookery Pond. Whether she has now become the White Lady of the Fire Station is not certain.

Perhaps the Spaniard of Crockwell is in fact a Cavalier in cloak and wide-brimmed hat, standing there waiting for his White Lady who will never come, unless, even more romantically, they have gone away somewhere to start a new afterlife together.

Mr Hedges tells an amusing story about a gardener at Bicester House who was going home from work late one night. Suddenly, in the dusk, he could just make out a woman dressed all in white, coming slowly but surely in his direction. He could hear the clip-clop of horses' hooves as well, getting nearer and nearer! The night was dark, he was alone, and he remembered all too well the story of the White Lady. He was terrified. As the White Lady came onwards, steadily onwards, towards him through the gloom, he felt as if his heart would burst inside him. Then he recognised the lady from the local dairy, in her white milking coat, with her cart full of churns.

Kidlington, sprawling along the main roads which run out of Oxford towards Banbury and the Midlands, some 5 miles from the city itself is almost a suburb. Best known for its being the home of Virgin millionaire Richard Branston, and its airport which trains pilots from all over the world, at first sight Kidlington appears to be constructed almost entirely of housing estates, a perfect example of ribbon development. In the heart of this, the largest village in England, however, lies an older Kidlington, centred on the High Street, Mill Street, and Church Street.

The 13th-century church of St Mary the Virgin stands in meadowland near the river Cherwell which makes its way towards the Thames at Oxford's Magdalen Bridge. St Mary's has for neighbours a row of gabled 17th-century almshouses, started soon after the Restoration. Each room is named after a member of the family of Sir William Morton, their founder - Madam Ann's Room, Madam Magdalen's Room, Mr John's Room, and so on.

Kidlington also has pleasant cottages, farmhouses, and its fair share of pubs, one of which is the Red Lion, on the main Oxford Road. The Red Lion was built in about 1960, and is typical of its era. No one has yet discovered what haunts the building, or why, but it must date from a time before the present Red Lion occupied the site. These happenings started in the late 1960's, and increased gradually in intensity until the early 1970's. Doors would open and shut of their own accord, lights and heaters switch themselves on and off unaided, accompanied by an unnerving assortment of strange bumps and bangs. One Sunday night, after closing time, the licensees, Mr and Mrs McC, were upstairs when they heard the telephone extension in the bar being picked up. Their son rushed downstairs immediately, only to find - nothing! He had his own strange experience to tell, and was of the opinion that whatever was in the pub uninvited had poltergeist tendencies. This was because, when he was in the bathroom one day, he distinctly saw a tin of talcum powder jump off a shelf and soar through the air into the bath.

According to the McC's, the strangest happening was the time when their Alsatian dog, Sabre, managed to become locked out of the pub overnight. Everyone had gone to bed, and the Red Lion was securely locked up for the night as usual, with Sabre safely inside it as he always was. When the family came down in the morning, the poor animal was sitting outside the locked door.

The McC's attempted to discover something about the site of the Red Lion, and found out that it had been used at times as a fairground site. To further their investigations the family allowed an Indian medium to come to their home to see if he could contact any sort of force in the vicinity, but to no avail.

A 1978 terraced council house. on the development known as the Moors, was the setting for another Kidlington haunting. Between the house's construction and 1982, three families moved out. The fourth family, however, were determined to stay and brave it out. They called in a priest to deal with their unwanted visitor.

Over a period of about two years, a series of weird and not very pleasant happenings were experienced by different members of the household. The first was the sound of a small baby crying, which proved to be nothing to do with children of the family. This noise lasted 'for ages.' Soon afterwards, the 2-year-old son saw a strange man going upstairs and, although he did not seem at all frightened, the boy insisted that his father go and look for the man.

Their 7-year-old daughter also saw a man, this time sitting hunched up on her bed. Not a nice thing for any young child to find, but worse was to come, for the man put his hand over the girl's mouth.

Then, another night when the parents were in bed, the father put his hand down onto the floor by the side of the bed, but, instead of making contact with the carpet as he had expected, he felt the slow, steady pounding of a heartbeat. It was as if a body of some sort were lying there by the side of the bed. Later the same night, the mother awoke to find her husband missing from bed and discovered him curled up asleep in exactly the same spot were the heart had been ticking away. She noted that he was curled up like a baby in the womb.

Some of the noises, particularly that of the crying baby, were also heard by visitors and neighbours, none of whom had been told about these sounds beforehand. Someone noticed that the happenings would start when the evenings began to draw out, and the longer days of spring had arrived.

One night, while the family was away, neighbours were disturbed by doors slamming in the haunted house. It is annoying enough to hear noises in the night coming from an adjoining terraced house, but ten times worse to hear them in an empty one. Not surprisingly, a neighbour decided to call in a priest to perform an exorcism and this seemed to have the desired effect, unless someone has evidence to the contrary.

In nearby **Gosford**, the King's Arms public house has a ghost story which dates back at least to 1976, the year in which the landlady, Mrs JD, spoke about the haunting to a reporter from the *Oxford Mail* who was writing an article on haunted hostelries. The present King's Arms is a modern building of honey-coloured stone, but designed to offer an old-world atmosphere. In 1976, however, before the pub was 'tarted up', as the reporter put it, Mrs D was well aware of a `feeling, a sort of cold feeling,' and footsteps. It has been suggested that the ghost is that of a Mother Louse, an imposing 17th-century landlady, who was famous for both her strong ale and her forceful personality. She also made excellent puddings and pies, which tempted customers from as far away as Oxford. The old King's Arms was nicknamed Louse Hall, hardly the ideal name for an inn, but this seems to have been no deterrent to customers. The sensation of being haunted was confirmed by both Mr and Mrs D, a temporary under-manager and his wife who were being trained in the licensing trade at the pub. They stated that they were definitely conscious of a `feeling' and used to hear footsteps, perhaps Mother Louse herself carrying out a quality control exercise.

Kirtlington, about 10 miles north of Oxford, was a centre of administration in Saxon times. It was a royal manor and, in the 11th century, belonged to Edward the Confessor, the Oxfordshire king who was born at Islip. Saxon stones are believed to lie under the chancel of the present church, which also has a solid Norman tower and a Tree of Life dating from the same period. The remains of a 13th-century wall painting show St George preparing to attack a red dragon. In 1658, Christopher Wren was buried here, the father of a more famous son of the same name, an Oxford Professor of Astronomy who was to become the greatest of English architects.

The village is dominated by its Park, a stately home constructed between 1742 and 1746 for Sir James Dashwood. It contains, among other interesting items, the fascinating Monkey Room, painted in 1745 by Clermont and depicting monkeys playing the part of huntsmen in a chase scene. The Park itself was landscaped by Capability Brown, and is now known as a leading polo venue, attended by the Prince of Wales.

Sir James Dashwood, the builder of Kirtlington Park, died in 1779, and his burial is recorded in the parish registers for 20th November that year. Sir James is said to have haunted both Park and village until his ghost was laid in a nearby pond. As is usual with such spirits, he will walk again if ever the pond is allowed to dry up.

Souldern, situated on the Oxfordshire-Northamptonshire border, about 5 miles east of Deddington, is one of the county's picture-postcard villages. Built mainly of local stone, it has a village pond, a Norman church and a rectory which features in a sonnet by Wordsworth, *A Parsonage in Oxfordshire*. Wordsworth's rectory is, alas, no more, and has been replaced by a Victorian one.

In the 1840's, a former Souldern resident aroused a considerable amount of interest when his or her skeleton was unearthed lying in a roughly made grave. It is believed to be that of an Anglo-Saxon who lived during the 5th or 6th century. The body was buried with some pots, ornaments, which could be bone earrings, and a wood and metal bucket. Roman coins have also turned up in the area and centuries later William the Conqueror gave the manor of Souldern to one of his followers. A later lord of the manor was the first Duke of Suffolk, William de la Pole, husband of Chaucer's daughter, Alice, who is buried in Ewelme church.

The Souldern haunting, a very personal affair, happened many years ago. On the night of 28th July, 1706, just before midnight, the Rector, Reverend Geoffrey Shaw, was sitting peacefully in his study, enjoying the summer night and having a quiet read and smoke before he turned in for the night. Imagine his surprise, then, when his relaxation was suddenly interrupted by the quite inexplicable appearance of his old friend, Master Nailor, former Vicar of Enstone. Apart from the lateness of the hour, the most extraordinary aspect of the visit was the fact that the Reverend Nailor was dead. He had died two years previously in his 49th year. Surprisingly calm under the circumstances, Reverend Shaw asked his dead visitor to take a seat and the ghost did so willingly. It then started to inform its friend that it had something of great importance to tell him, something of a personal nature. The phantom confided in Rev Shaw that a certain mutual friend from their Cambridge days, a Mr Orchard, would die very suddenly, and worse still, that Geoffrey Shaw himself was due to follow him to the grave. The Rector was warned, therefor, to prepare himself for the next world. This visitation lasted about two hours, during which the Rector took the opportunity of asking Master Nailor if it were possible to gain any insight into the nature and workings of the afterlife from one's experience in this one. The answer was a straight, 'No,' but the spirit did admit to being itself, 'well and happy.' Rev Shaw then asked if any of their old friends were already with him on the other side, and on being informed that they were not, felt, 'struck to the heart.'

The ghostly Master Nailor left at the end of his allotted period, explaining that there were only three days made available for 'leave of absence' and that these had all but expired. He also mentioned that it would not be possible for the two friends to meet again before Rev Shaw's own demise. As predicted, Mr Orchard did die suddenly in his chair at St John's College, Cambridge, on 6th August that year, 'while his bed-maker was gone to fetch his commons for supper.' As for the Reverend Shaw, he obediently died as instructed by the ghost. This happened a few weeks after the visitation, while he was reading the Lesson at Evensong in Souldern church. He was buried the following day, very near the spot where he had dropped down dead. The doctors said that, just like poor Arthur Orchard, Mr Shaw had died of apoplexy, 'of the same distemper,' as they put it.

Weston on the Green is an attractive little place, with thatched cottages and Norman church, and lies about 8 miles north of Oxford on the Northampton road. It is the setting for a haunting at the Weston Manor Hotel, which was once a monastery, and is now a fine hotel with historical features. These include a ghostly nun and possibly two other spectres, all included in the price of a room. In 1973, Mr Nicholas Price, the proprietor, talked to a reporter from the *Bicester Advertiser* about the hotel ghosts and the manor itself. The building was founded in the 11th century, and the present buildings date from the 14th, with additions from the 16th and 19th centuries. The ancient moat now serves as a swimming pool, and the former chapel, situated at the end of the Great Hall, is used as a conference room. The so-called Minstrels' Gallery, which overlooks the Hall, was in fact the solar, and used by the Abbot of Osney, (the manor of Weston being owned by that abbey), as a sort of vantage point from which to supervise the payment of tythes which took place in the Hall below.

The Manor's best authenticated ghost is known locally as Mad Maude and she is said to have been a 13th-century nun from a nearby convent. In the time-honoured way, she was involved in a love affair with a monk from the monastery, and was discovered one night in her lover's cell. Found guilty of breaking her vow of chastity, Maude was made an example of and condemned to be burnt at the stake in the grounds of the Manor. Not surprisingly, this harsh sentence unhinged her mind, and caused her to find no rest in this world or the next. It is uncertain, however, whether the punishment was actually carried out. Mr Price was convinced that Maude returned to Weston, the scene of so much emotion, and that her favourite haunt is the Oak Bedroom, a beautiful room and most suitable for this sort of story, with oak panelling, beams and four-poster bed.

One guest in particular seems to have been greatly affected by the feeling of gloom and terror which permeates that room and, while staying at the Manor on a course, demanded to be given another bedroom, despite the fact that, as course leader, he had been allotted the Oak Room as the finest in the hotel. He had woken up sensing an overwhelming sensation of something menacing in the room with him, although he could see nothing in the darkness. He could not be persuaded to set foot in the room again during his stay at Weston Manor. Other guests have experienced a very unpleasant feeling in this lovely bedroom, but no one has apparently been able to see anything to account for it.

Local tradition speaks of a phantom coach which races through the hotel grounds. It comes into the yard, only to disappear immediately, but no evidence, either historical or legendary, gives any reason for its being there. Mr Price, who has carried out some investigation into the matter, mentioned that an elderly man who used to work in the hotel gardens, would take a very long way round in order to avoid any chance of seeing the spectral coach.

Mr Price also suspected that he may have seen another ghost on the premises, that of a dairymaid who fell to her death in the tower. At the bottom of the steps, there is a wooden floor which bears a mark supposed to be a bloodstain which cannot be removed. As a dairymaid is unlikely to have had any business being in the tower, it is surmised that she committed suicide.

Yarnton lies just off the A34, 5 miles north west of Oxford. In the 16th century, The village was the home of a branch of the Spencers of Althorp, the family of Diana, Princess of Wales. It is an attractive little place, its principal treasures being the Jacobean manor house, built by Sir Thomas Spencer in 1612, and the fine Norman church. The same Sir Thomas rebuilt the church tower and St Bartholomew's is noted for its gallery of stained glass. The most unusual subjects are seven little birds, each with a comment. The owl, for example, says, 'Ye shall pray for the Fox.' The Spencer chapel is particularly splendid with its coloured ceiling, blue with gilded stars. Here lie two life-size figures of Sir Thomas, 1608, and Sir William, 1648. Every year on 4th January, the church tolls its great bell 87 times, one stroke for every year of the life of the village's greatest benefactor, Alderman William Fletcher, who died in 1827. He gave Yarnton its primary school, endowed village charities, and donated valuable art treasures to the church.

Yarnton is known for its water meadows which have never been under the plough, and so offer an exceptional range of wild flowers. The owners of the meadows appoint two 'meadsmen' who, as their predecessor did for countless generations, auction off the grazing and mowing rights. Formerly these meadows were divided up into lots called 'mowths' and after the auction lots were drawn for their distribution. This involved the use of thirteen balls made of cherry wood, each bearing the name of a mowth, such as William of Bladon, or Watery Mollie. Today the rights are sold to just one taker so that he is able to work them economically using modern farming methods.

Yarnton Manor is now the Oxford Centre for Post-Graduate Hebrew Studies, and looks every inch the haunted house. One Yarnton villager said, in the sort of voice which implied that everyone should know all about the subject, 'Oh, but it *is* haunted. She's a maidservant who is supposed to have committed suicide there. I don't know the details, but we all knew about her when we went to school there.' Part of the Manor House was once used as a schoolroom when she was a girl.

Another annual event is reputed to take place on 3rd June, in a field on the outskirts of the village, when Royalist troops are to be seen busily making their escape from besieged Oxford, and hurrying off to the safety of the Midlands.

Yarnton's other haunted spot is neither ancient nor romantic. It is a signal box. A railway worker called Tom Stone arrived there for an evening shift, and, because no trains were expected for a full half-hour, he was looking forward to relaxing in the calm of a sunny evening. Suddenly, he heard someone walking along the boards underneath where he was sitting. The signal box was not at all creepy, so Tom was annoyed rather than scared at the idea of his solitude being interrupted. Then heavy footsteps began to climb slowly up the outside stairs. The door handle was firmly grasped, then turned, and the door itself shaken hard as if someone were trying to force their way in. Tom waited impatiently. He did not want company and wondered who was just about to disturb him in this way. Nothing and nobody entered. He waited a minute or two longer, but no one came or left the box. The only thing he noticed was a very strong and distinctive smell of tobacco. He seemed to be alone with the tobacco and the echo of those heavy footsteps. In some strange way, he seemed to recognise both smell and sound, in fact they reminded him of a former senior porter. The only factor which prevents this from being a classic case of haunting, is that the phantom visitor, although retired from the railway, was still very much alive and well!

CHAPTER FIVE:
SOUTH OXFORDSHIRE

Tourist Information Centres:
Didcot: The Car Park, Station Road, Didcot, OX11 7AU
Tel: 01235 813243
Henley on Thames: Town Hall, Market Place, Henley, RG9 2AQ
Tel: 01491 578034
Thame: Market House, North Street, Thame, OX9 3HH
Tel: 01844 212834
Wallingford: Town Hall, Market Place, Wallingford, OX10 0EG
Tel: 01491 826972

The ghosts of South Oxfordshire are far from being mere vague shapes or unaccounted-for footsteps: they have names, are well documented and live on in the histories of their own towns and villages. Outstanding among Oxfordshire ghosts are the ladies of this region: the lovely Sarah Fletcher at Clifton Hampden, the 'very big woman' at Holton Park, sinister Mary Blandy at Henley and Lady Arabella of Rycote.

The church at **Beckley**, one of the 'towns' of Otmoor, was the setting for a strange occurrence related to the exposé of misappropriation of funds. A plate on the church wall recorded the gift of money destined for a village charity. One day this plate was found to be missing, along with the relevant cash. Shortly afterwards the vicar followed them, and one of the churchwardens was suspected of foul play.

Church services were then disturbed by the latch of the church door rattling, and noises from the roof which sounded like 'hundreds of marbles rolling on the leads.' The congregation dashed outside, but passers-by had seen nothing amiss. Beckley villagers claimed that the benefactor was pointing out the theft and sure enough, when the charity began to function once again, the disruptions stopped.

Named after the family which gave John Hampden to English history, **Clifton Hampden** is a small village of timbered and thatched cottages, sited on the Thames, 7 miles south of Oxford. Its main attractions are its flowers and its river, peaceful under the canopies which the trees throw over the Thames here. The small church perches on a rock, high above the river, and in its churchyard is a memorial to the man who fired the first shot at the Battle of Waterloo.

Although, until the county boundary changes of 1974, the village was in Berkshire, its famous old inn, the Barley Mow, was always in Oxfordshire. Apart from its own natural attributes, and its general air of knowing what the discerning visitor is looking for in a traditional village pub, the Barley Mow was immortalised by Jerome K Jerome in 1889 in his novel, Three Men in a Boat. Although the building was very badly damaged by fire in 1975, it has been restored to all of its former thatched loveliness.

The Plough, at the junction of the road which leads into the village from the main road, has what was described as an invisible presence in the Oxford Mail, 19th October 1966, but this pales into insignificance compared with the very visible figure of Sarah Fletcher, who haunts the Barley Mow car park and certain other venues in Clifton Hampden.

In the south aisle of Dorchester Abbey, not far from the font, is a memorial slab inscribed as follows:

Reader! If thou Hast a heart fam'd for tenderness and Pity, Contemplate this Spot. In which are deposited the remains of a Young Lady whose artless Beauty, innocence of Mind and gentle manners, once obtained her the Love and Esteem of all who knew her. But when Nerves were too delicately spun to bear the rude Shakes and Jostlings which we meet with in this transitory World, Nature gave way: She sunk and died a Martyr to Excessive Sensibility. Mrs Sarah Fletcher, wife of Capt. Fletcher, departed this life at the village of Clifton on the 7th of June, 1799. In the 29 year of her Age.

At the end of the eighteenth century, the village was the home of Sarah, a lovely lady in her late twenties, who was happily married to a sea-captain and lived in a large Georgian house. In 1799, however, Sarah's life was torn apart when she discovered that her beloved husband had attempted to arrange a bigamous marriage to an heiress. Unable to cope with this dreadful news, she committed suicide by hanging herself on the bed rail. She did this on 7th June, 1799, and an inquest took place on the following day, the verdict being that she had taken her own life while the balance of her mind was disturbed. The Coroner's report, dated 8th June, and

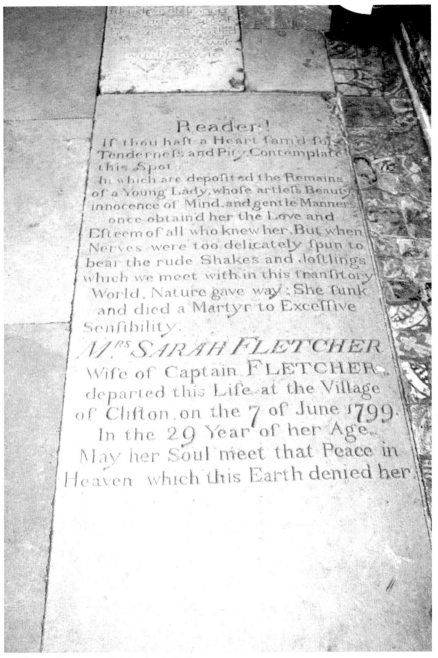

Reader!
If thou haft a Heart fam'd for
Tendernefs and Pity,Contemplate
this Spot.
In which are depofited the Remains
of a Young Lady,whofe artlefs Beauty
innocence of Mind,and gentle Manners
once obtain'd her the Love and
Efteem of all who knew her,But when
Nerves were too delicately fpun to
bear the rude Shakes and Joftlings
which we meet with in this tranfitory
World, Nature gave way : She funk
and died a Martyr to Exceffive
Senfibility.

M^{RS} SARAH FLETCHER
Wife of Captain FLETCHER,
departed this Life at the Village
of Clifton, on the 7 of June 1799.
In the 29 Year of her Age.
May her Soul meet that Peace in
Heaven which this Earth denied her.

Dorchester Abbey, memorial slab to Sarah Fletcher

preserved in Oxfordshire County Archives, under the Quarter Session returns for Trinity, 1799, returns a verdict of 'Lunacy', the costs being £1 for the entry and 6 shillings for the travelling 8 miles out from Oxford. The report is signed by C Willoughby, Chairman, of whom more later.

Dorchester Abbey burial register shows no entry for Sarah's interment there, even though the slab states quite clearly that she lies there. The Clifton Hampden register, however, includes a bald statement: 1799, May 10th, Fletcher, Sarah. No mention of suicide, or burial at Dorchester, but the fact that, according to this, she was buried a month before she died! Perhaps it is this carelessness with the dates, or the description of herself as insane, when she had very good cause to lose her reason, or the fact that her husband's attempt at committing serious crime is not recorded for posterity, that makes Sarah walk. She is one of the most active and well documented of all Oxfordshire ghosts, having appeared for about two centuries. Her story has appeared in the Didcot Advertiser 2nd January 1959, and the Wallingford Herald, 24th October 1963, and first hand accounts are known. Her walking came up, quite casually, in a conversation about Clifton Hampden as recently as November 2000, when someone happened to mention that he had once lived in the village. Sarah has been sighted at regular intervals ever since her death, both inside her old home, and out and about in Clifton Hampden. On the anniversary of her death, she has been spotted on several occasions gazing mournfully from her bedroom window. She is easily identified by her distinctive auburn hair, which she wears tied round with a violet ribbon, and in recent years she has been reported as wearing a very romantic long black velvet cloak, which suits her colouring admirably.

Some fifty years after her death, Sarah appeared quite frequently in order to visit a country parson, the Reverend Edward Crake, to whom she seems to have taken quite a fancy. Mr Crake, a bachelor, lived as a young man with his parents at Sarah's old home where they ran a boarding school and so far reciprocated her attentions that he fell in love with her. Far from being afraid of his phantom love, he is reported as saying,

"Romance came to me by candlelight and with my eyes held to hers, I saw once more the perfection of Sarah Fletcher's beauty. At any rate, she was no dark spirit of evil."

The other members of his family, and later residents of the house, were not quite so enthusiastic about her visitations, possibly because they were sometimes rather noisy.

Clifton Hampden, The Barley Mow

Miss L, wrote in March 1984 about how she had come across Sarah on the Christmas Eve of 1970. She had been out for a drink at the Barley Mow with a male friend and, not being familiar with Clifton Hampden and the immediate vicinity, had not heard of Sarah's existence, alive or dead. Miss L only recognised Sarah as a ghost some three years or so after her experience, when she was talking to the Vicar of Clifton Hampden, who told her the full story. She was also informed by an elderly resident of the village that Sarah takes a certain route, and the place where Miss L saw her in 1970 formed part of it.

On the evening in question, Miss L and her friend left the Barley Mow about 9 o'clock, and made their way to where they had left their car in the pub car park. They noticed that theirs was the only car there and they were positive that no other customers were about as they walked towards the vehicle. They got in and remarked on the fact that there was a full moon that night. Miss L then noticed what appeared to be the moon taking up virtually all the space in the passenger window of the car. It did strike her as very odd that the moon had changed its position so rapidly and was now on their left instead of the right. As she was asking herself how this could be possible, she realised that the 'moon' was in fact a pale face, pressed up close against her window. It was the face of a young woman and, apart from its sudden appearance out of nowhere, the most unnatural thing about it was that it appeared to be transparent. Miss L was quite taken with their unexpected visitor, and not in the least frightened, even though she knew that they were alone in the car park and that the lady had no obvious means of reaching them. Miss L gazed at Sarah, who gazed steadily back at Miss L; according to the Reverend Crake, she was adept at this sort of thing. This lasted about two minutes, during which time Miss L was struck by the fact that only the face was visible, nothing else of Sarah could she see at all. This could be explained by the black velvet cloak being hard to make out on a dark December night. The visitor was not at all menacing and Miss L stressed that she would have sat there quite happily all night and would have welcomed the chance to communicate with Sarah in some way, had not her companion lost his nerve and driven off, leaving poor Mrs Fletcher standing forlornly there, in the Barley Mow car park, on Christmas Eve. Perhaps she is doomed to be for ever deserted, sad and alone in this world and the next, making her one of the most pathetic as well as the most interesting of our local ghosts.

Henley on Thames lies on the haunted A423, 23 miles south-east of Oxford, on the county's southernmost border with Berkshire. Henley lies in stockbroker country, with lovely river scenery backed by the wooded Chiltern Hills which dip down to meet the Thames at this point. The Henley area is home to a host of film, television, and musical celebrities, even an ex-Beatle, for George Harrison has a mansion just outside the town. It is probably best known for its annual regattas, the Royal which takes place in the first week of July, and the Town Regatta on the last Saturday of July, or the first one in August.

The town is fortunate in its interesting range of hotels and public houses, a legacy of the days when Henley was an important coaching centre. There are plenty of timbered buildings, bow-fronted boutiques and antique shops. Bell Street has both the sixteenth-century Bear, and the Bull, which dates from the previous century and claims to be the town's oldest inn. Its exact date, however, is uncertain, but it is known to have been in existence in 1478 when it was referred to as 'Le Boull'. It looks very much the part with its massive timber doorway which must have seen the arrival and departure of hundreds of stagecoaches. Regulars at the Bull have reported several instances of an unexplained smell of burnt candles, which always comes from exactly the same spot, in the same bar. On one occasion, a resident saw a cowled figure which leaned over him when he was in bed.

The Kenton Theatre, which opened in 1805, is in New Street and is one of England's oldest theatres still being used for its original purpose. Any attempt to close it down has been met with strenuous opposition from local people, notably Jeremy Irons, who lives at Watlington. In the late 1960's, a local playwright, Miss Joan Morgan, wrote *The Hanging Wood*, based on the life of a Henley girl, Mary Blandy, who was hanged on 6th March, 1752, on the castle Mound at Oxford, for poisoning her father, the lawyer, Francis Blandy.

What happened in the Blandy case has been told in a pamphlet which Mary herself wrote, in the form of a letter, while in Oxford Gaol awaiting execution, and several letters written by her, her lover, and others involved in the affair, survive; some of these are kept in the Public Record Office. In addition, a number of illustrated accounts of her crime and its consequences have appeared in print.

This is the gist of them. Francis Blandy seems to have been an amiable but incautious little man who was very fond of his daughter, Mary. He unwisely let it be known in the Henley area that, when she married, her husband could expect to receive £10,000, and he encouraged her to spurn any suitors whom father and daughter considered to be of unsuitable social standing. Rejects included the Parish Clerk of Henley, Edward Herne.

No better offer was forthcoming, however, and at the advanced age of 30, Miss Blandy found herself still unmarried, and rapidly becoming panic stricken lest she be left on the shelf. Then, by some miracle, she made the acquaintance of a certain Scottish soldier, William Cranstoun. He was rumoured to have connexions with the aristocracy, and was therefore looked on as suitable for Mary's hand, and cash, at last. Cranstoun had, in his turn, heard about the sum intended for Mary's husband, and so he came a-courting.

Gradually, though, doubts began to intrude themselves into the mind of Mary's doting father, concerning the character of his prospective son-in-law. Cranstoun, it appeared, did not improve with closer acquaintance; he had already shown himself a traitor to his native land by fighting in the Hanoverian army at Culloden. Worse, far worse, was the fact that he was, so Mr Blandy heard, already married, in 1744, to an Anne Murray. If that were not enough, he was deep in debt and, it transpired later, had an illegitimate daughter by another lady. Accordingly, Mr Blandy threw Cranstoun out of the house, and he went willingly enough, but neither man had reckoned on the determination of the bride-to-be. No longer a spring chicken, particularly by the standards of the age, she knew full well that her Willie represented the last chance she might have of ever marrying, and now that he was in her clutches she had no intention of releasing him. Not to please her father, or all the citizens of Henley put together, were he to leave Henley, and marry him she would. So Willie stayed on, and the couple began to scheme.

Shortly afterwards, Willie announced one morning over breakfast that he had seen Francis Blandy's ghost. Wasn't that odd? Could Mr Blandy be ill? So saying, he began to sow the seeds of doubt in the elderly man's mind concerning his own health. Then Willie left for Scotland, but not before, as was later revealed, he had managed to doctor Mr Blandy's tea with a strange powder. Very soon, the lawyer began to feel decidedly unwell.

After that, a package arrived for Mary from her Willie up in Scotland. It contained some Scottish pebbles, together with some powder which was to be used for polishing them. Some of this powder found its way into her

Divinity School, Oxford, scene of Mary Blandy's trial

father's tea, with the result that he felt even more unwell. Also affected was the maid, Susannah Gunnel, who had helped herself to some leftover tea. Mr Blandy, though, was not yet beaten.

Another letter arrived from Cranstoun, this time advising Mary to clean her pebbles with the powder mixed in gruel rather than tea, obviously because the wretched Mr Blandy obstinately refused to die. Susannah was instructed to make up some gruel, and Mary was seen to mix in some of the powder herself. She was unwise enough to warn the maids not to eat any of the mixture, "or else it would be the worse for them." Mary even asked, "Who would grudge to send an old father to hell for the sake of £10,000?", a remark which did not endear her to the staff. Susannah saw fit to pass on this gem of daughterly devotion to the 'old father', who, silly little man, only murmured, "poor love-sick girl!" At last, realising her indiscretions, the 'girl' threw the powder, together with the letters from Cranstoun, onto the fire, but in her haste to be rid of them, did not ensure that they had caught light. Susannah Gunnel, on the other hand, was intelligent enough to snatch the evidence from the fire and took the powder round to the nearest chemist to have it identified. It proved to be arsenic.

Three days later Mr Blandy did die, and the doctor who attended him promptly locked Mary into her room, and posted her rejected suitor, Mr Herne, outside on sentry duty. At this point the story takes on all the elements of a farce. Herne was then called away to dig Mr Blandy's grave. Mary seized this opportunity to escape, which she did by running half-dressed into the street. The people of Henley, no doubt alerted by Susannah Gunnel, set on her immediately, and she was forced to find refuge in the Angel Inn, but was presently removed and packed off to Oxford.

The prisoner was brought to stand trial in the Divinity School, now part of the Bodleian Library, and found guilty as charged, despite her plea that she had believed the powder to be some sort of love potion that she had given to her father so that he might grow to love her once again after their differences over the Cranstoun affair.

It was six weeks before she was hanged, and she spent the time writing a long account of her own version of Mr Blandy's illness and subsequent decease. When the day of execution, 6th March, finally arrived, Mary gave the hangman two guineas and requested that she be not hanged too high, 'for decency'. Her body was brought back to Henley, and buried by Edward Herne in a coffin lined with white satin, in a grave next to her father.

A warrant was issued for the arrest of Cranstoun, but he managed to escape to Flanders, where he died in the December of the same year, 1752.

Ironically, when Mr Blandy's will was read, it was found that the little lawyer's entire estate amounted to only £4,000, so the figure named as a marriage portion was either a figment of his imagination, or wishful thinking.

To return to the Kenton Theatre, Mr Henderson, one of the co-directors of *The Hanging Wood*, said that as soon as rehearsals got under way, all sorts of strange incidents started to happen: lights switched themselves on and off; doors opened and closed by themselves, and, most startling of all, a large mirror suddenly jumped off the wall. It did not break immediately, but sat there on the floor for some seconds, then shattered as if it had been dealt a sudden, hard blow. In addition, a cup flew up into the air and smashed, just as Mary Blandy's name was being mentioned.

After this, people became aware of a strange female figure standing at the rear of the theatre while the rehearsals were in progress. No one recognised her as anyone they knew, and she was never seen to enter or leave the building by any conventional route, despite careful observation on the part of the members of the theatre company.

The Blandy case was familiar to the people of Henley, and several years previously an enactment of the trial was being performed at the Town Hall. Strange to relate, a similar female figure had been seen loitering in the building, just as if she were taking an interest in the performance. The cast of *The Hanging Wood* was not unduly perturbed by their visitor at the Kenton Theatre, because it is generally considered lucky for a theatre to be haunted, hence perhaps the expression 'the ghost walks' for pay day.

In November 2001, the *South Oxfordshire Courier* carried a front-page article on the Henley hauntings; professional ghost-busting had been employed to look into the case, but with a total lack of success.

The **Long Wittenham** area has been inhabited since at least the Iron Age as local forts and barrows prove. The village lies off the A 415, 8 miles south of Oxford. Its church was built in the 1120's of stone brought there from Caen in Normandy, and is the third to occupy the site. Its rare lead font shows thirty bishops in the act of conferring blessings, and had a very narrow escape from being melted down to make bullets, thanks to its being hidden in a wooden casing. The most unusual treasure of the church is a piscina which consists of a quatrefoil basin combined with a miniature effigy of a knight. Wearing armour which dates him from the early14th century, he is only 2 feet long, and remains unidentified.

The village also has a Saxon cross, St Anthony's Well which is said to have healing powers, a 13th-century cruck cottage, the ruins of a cockpit, and fishponds and dovecote, the latter both reminders of the time when fish was virtually compulsory on Fridays, and fresh meat was scarce in winter.

At Long Wittenham, a long-standing village ghost story tells of a phantom coach and four which rushes along by the Old Manor House. If anyone is in the vicinity, it is essential for him to whistle as loud as humanly possible in order to drown the noise that it makes, for to hear it means certain death.

About a month before Christmas 1962, strange and inexplicable happenings shook the staff of the Oxford and District Co-operative Society's grocery stores in the High Street. It started one Monday evening when the manager, Mr DA Bird, returned to the shop after going home for his evening meal. The Christmas lights in the front window of the shop were not working and he had come back to repair them. When he returned, however, they were twinkling away as if there was nothing at all wrong with them.

On the Tuesday evening, Mr and Mrs Bird were working late. He told the *Oxford Mail* reporter, 'I thought I saw something come from behind the counter,' as they both worked in the shop window. The Birds turned round at the same moment, sensing, 'a gush of nothing.' Then, at 9.15, the fairy lights suddenly went out.

The following morning, Mr Bird and an assistant, Mrs Joyce Stanier, discovered two boxes of porridge oats placed neatly on the shop floor in front of the door to the storeroom. In addition, three boxes of cereals had migrated to the section where cleaning materials were on display, and four small tubs of bicarbonate of soda had found their way to a window sill where the children's books were kept.

Because 9 o'clock in the evening seemed to be the peak time for 'happenings', all the shop staff assembled at the back of the premises, ready and waiting for any activity which might take place. The main shop lights were switched off between 9.10 and 9.25, and only the fairy lights left on. Then, at 9.15, these turned themselves off, but, when told to come on again

Long Wittenham

by Mr Bird, did so obediently. Everyone in the shop sensed a strange presence there, and heard noises in the front section despite its being locked.

By the Thursday, the entire staff was beginning to feel the strain, and so they agreed to spend the evening playing bingo to take their minds off what had been going on. Nevertheless, they couldn't resist going back to the shop afterwards, and they all went in together. At first everything seemed quite normal. Then someone spotted that the porridge boxes had returned to their position on the floor.

Enough was enough, and Mr Bird called the Co-op's head office in Oxford. The grocery manager, a Mr Styles, and security officers arrived Friday evening and carried out a thorough examination of the premises. The wiring had already been checked by electricians as being the most obvious cause.

Mr Bird told the reporter, 'I don't know what is happening. We are not hysterical, but the coincidences are uncanny.' Mrs Stanier was more outspoken. 'If it is a practical joker at work, I think he is a despicable coward.' she said. 'But there are many things happening of which there is no logical explanation. I don't know how I will carry on if it does not stop.'

She added that although she was unwilling to credit a ghost with all that had happened, there was a tale in Long Wittenham about a phantom old lady who would walk from a large house nearby, past the back of the Co-op and on to the church. As recent building work had disturbed her route, perhaps she was giving vent to her annoyance.

Marsh Baldon, one of 'The Baldons', as the signposts indicate - the other is Toot Baldon - is a pleasant little place south east of Oxford between the haunted A423 and the B480. Marsh Baldon is grouped around a large green. The village was once made up mainly of timbered and thatched buildings, but many of these have been destroyed by fire over the years. Nevertheless, it still has a variety of styles and building materials to attract the visitor, and many of the houses and cottages are distinctive. The village school is one of the oldest in the neighbourhood; it was given to Marsh Baldon in the middle of the eighteenth century.

St Peter's church has an ancient sundial, possibly as old as 12th-century, and inside the church are a Jacobean pulpit, some interesting glass and the arms of Henry VIII. A large picture under the tower arch was given in 1794 by a Lord of the Manor and local magistrate, Sir Christopher Willoughby.

Marsh Baldon

Marsh Baldon is the scene of what appears to be a regular haunting, the ghost concerned being that of the same Sir Christopher Willoughby who donated the painting to the church. It will be remembered that he was also the magistrate who signed the Coroner's report on the suicide of Sarah Fletcher of Clifton Hampden. According to local sources, Sir Christopher continues to take his constitutional, smartly dressed as in life, in a long coat with shiny buttons. He walks from the Manor, and makes his way along the lane by the church, as if he has yet to realise that he died at the beginning of the 19th century.

Rycote Chapel stands in the grounds of Rycote Park, off the B4013, about 10 miles east of Oxford. The park was the site of a 16th-century mansion belonging to the Norreys family, a Civil War battle was fought at Rycote, but the house was not burnt down until the 18th century.

The Chapel of St Michael and All Angels was built for one of the Lords of the Manor of Rycote, Richard Quatremayne, whose table tomb can be seen in Thame church a few miles away. Completed in 1449, the chapel is unusual in that it is all of the same building period, and has not been added to structurally since the 15th century. The majority of the pews are contemporary with the building, but a couple of them are rather startling 17th-century additions, one with a canopy, the other with a minstrels' gallery.

Several visits have been paid by royalty over the centuries, including those of Elizabeth I, who attended a service there in 1592, James I, who came in 1616, Charles I who rode over from Oxford in 1625.

Old as the chapel itself is, a tree which stands beside it is said to be much older. If the date attributed to it is correct, it was planted in the reign of King Stephen, in the 12th century.

The last owners put the chapel in the care of the then Ministry of Works, and £45,000 was spent on restoring it so that now it can be seen in its original splendour as in the time of Richard Quatremayne.

In 1968, the Custodian, Mr Clifford Morris, local writer and poet, grew to have such an affinity with his place of work that the chapel's resident ghost, the Grey Lady, came to visit him. Just as he was preparing to lock up and go home one December afternoon, she made her appearance. She looked exactly as she is described in the ancient legend which tells of her existence. She wore a grey dress, but Mr Morris was unable to catch a glimpse of her face. Two years previously, by some strange coincidence, he had written a poem about her, and this had included a description of her in the grey dress, and mentioned the fact that no one had been privileged to see her face. If their meeting was a case of the wish being father to the event, it is odd that he had taken two years or more to conjure her up. After he had seen her, the custodian sat down and added an extra verse to his poem, as a sort of welcome back to "Lady Arabella" as he addressed her. Although a couple of visiting dogs were heard to growl, and their hair stood on end for no apparent reason, she had not appeared again by the time Mr Morris was interviewed by the *Oxford Mail*, 25th August 1969, despite his poetic invitation for her to return to visit him.

Mr Morris is by no means the only person to have seen Arabella. There seems to be considerable differences of opinion as to her identity, but suggestions made over the years include Lady Jane Grey, although this may well refer to the colour of her dress.

Thame, on the A418, 13 miles east of Oxford, is, as the locals say, "Thame by name and tame by nature", a reference to the pronunciation of the town's name. It had its origins in an Anglo-Saxon settlement by the River Thame, which was stimulated by a weekly market for which the charter was granted in the 1180's by the Bishop of Lincoln in whose huge diocese the town then lay. He altered the road through the town in order to direct all traffic into the market place, and developed a new settlement known as New Thame. Both Old and New Thame are situated at the western end of the High Street, clustered round the church and the Prebendal. The market place, which takes up part of both the Upper and Lower High Streets, is one of the widest in the country.

Just past Priest End, off the Lower High Street, is Church Road with its half-timbered almshouses, a timber framed 16th-century tithe barn, and the original buildings of Lord Williams's Grammar School. The church of St Mary the Virgin stands on a Saxon site, and is like a cathedral in miniature. Although the present fabric is mainly thirteenth-century, it offers fine examples of architectural styles down the ages. The interior has several interesting tombs, including those of Lord and Lady Williams, who lie in state in the chancel as fine alabaster effigies, and the table tombs of the Quatremayne family from Rycote and North Weston. There are also good brasses, one of them showing Geoffrey Dormer, a fifteenth-century merchant, his two wives and twenty five children. St Mary's is haunted by a grey lady, although who or what she was, no one seems to know.

In Lower High Street is the Old Trout restaurant, which bears on its colour washed frontage the date c1550. In the 1960's, when the restaurant was known as the Olde Thatche, the people of Thame were surprised to hear, out of the blue, that the Thatche had suddenly become the home of an Elizabethan priest. This obliging clergyman, it was reported, even lent a hand with the washing-up when the need arose. It was puzzling that nothing had been heard of him until then and that, when a certain amount of scepticism had been expressed, he never appeared again.

In the 16th century, the Manor of Thame was bought by Lord Williams, one time warden of the future Queen Elizabeth while she was still a princess and appeared as a threat to the throne of her half-sister, 'Bloody Mary' Tudor. Williams endowed the almshouses and founded the grammar school. One of its pupils was John Hampden who came back to Thame to die at the Greyhound, after being mortally wounded at the battle of Chalgrove Field, in 1643. Hampden is buried in his native Buckinghamshire, but he is said to reinact after death his last journey while still alive. His ghost, they say, comes back to Thame in June, and there are those who claim to have heard the slow hoof beats of his mount as it comes along Buttermarket to Hampden House, the successor of the Greyhound, where a wall plaque commemorates the event.

A haunted building right in the heart of Thame is the Bird Cage pub in Cornmarket, a half-timbered, fairytale place. Its origins, though, were not so pleasant, for it was built as a debtors' prison by the Bishop of Lincoln, then, during the Napoleonic Wars, French prisoners were kept there. The *Oxford Times,* of 25th December (sic) 1981, writes that the pub's ghost might be that of a leper who was pulled off the street into a ground floor room, in order to save him from a street mob who were stoning him. The landlords, Mr and Mrs E, told the *Times* about a 'consistent drumming' on the wall which takes place between the hours of 2 and 4 in the morning, and about one of the upstairs rooms the atmosphere of which disturbs both of them whenever they have to go into it.

Although Mr E was not totally convinced, Mrs E insisted that she had the creeps by a spirit which she has named 'Ghosty Boy'. There seems no doubt, though, that the cellar, where the prisoners were actually confined, houses a definite 'something' which remains trapped in the Bird Cage after all these years.

Thame, the Birdcage

Another haunted Thame pub is the Oxford Arms. The K's, who moved in as licensees in the mid-1970's, told the *Oxford Times*, 28th May 1976, that they were not aware that they were likely to have to share their home with a phantom. The first they heard about it was the sound of glasses being clinked together in the night, just as if a couple of people were saying "Cheers!", as Mrs K put it. They heard the sound on subsequent nights after the bar was closed, but saw nothing. Then, one evening, as a friend was sitting in the public bar, he looked up and asked them, "Who just walked through behind the bar?" Then, once again, they heard the mysterious clink of glasses. Their friend had seen a shape walk through from the living quarters upstairs, through the bars and into the saloon bar. It had not been sufficiently distinct to say for certain whether it was male or female, but a human figure it was. Everyone agreed that there was surely something uncanny about the place. Several customers have been aware of strange and assorted noises in the Oxford Arms, but to date no one has been able to identify the ghost or come up with any good reason for its being on the premises.

A couple of miles from Thame, off the minor road which leads through to Milton Common and the M40, is the hamlet of **Moreton**. Although this tiny place has no church, it does have several lovely period cottages, a pub, a defunct non-conformist chapel, and. . . . Archibald.

Archibald haunts half-timbered Brook Cottage on the outskirts of Moreton, next to the bridge which leads off to Thame. Well away from the madding crowd, and no asset to anyone, Archibald is far more convincing than any tourist attraction type of ghost. Archibald, in fact, verged on the embarrassing. In the 1960's he was both seen and heard on occasions by several members of the owner's family, and also by a tenant. The owner's family was very down to earth and gave the distinct impression that Archibald was not their idea of fun.

Trouble came to a head when Mrs L moved into Brook Cottage. She started to decorate the place, but every five minutes or so a knock would come at the cottage door. When she got to the door and found there was no one to be seen, she was justifiably annoyed. Not only was it inconvenient, it was rather eerie in view of the remote situation. It was not long, however, before Mrs L started to see someone. The first time she saw Archibald was when she was putting out the milk bottles one night, and there he was, as she told the *Oxford Mail*, of 18th June 1962, a 'tall, whey-faced man, aged between 50 and 60, wearing a black cape and a black top hat.' Mrs L went on to say that he just stood looking at her without saying a word. She then decided that she would have to show him just who was boss, because she was going to be living at Brook Cottage, with or without Archibald's approval. She demonstrated this by marching straight past him as if she were not at all afraid. She said that at no time had she in fact been afraid of him, and her family took no notice of him.

On another occasion, Mrs L saw him again, this time in broad daylight, standing near the garage. A relative of the owner said that he too had seen a tall black figure wearing a top hat, go past the window one day.

The owner himself, Mr RQ, knew quite a bit about Archibald from first hand experience, and was able to add to Mrs L's account, in the *Oxford Mail*, 21st August 1962, and the *Thame Gazette*, 22nd August 1962. Mr Q had lived in Brook Cottage himself until the death of his wife when he moved to Thame. He added that a farmer had hanged himself on the premises about 1890, and that it was his ghost that revisited the place. Mr Q would hear him 'knocking about' in the house and he even came in twice while Mr Q was there one night. Mrs Q felt Archibald touch her leg. He then switched the lights off, then after the Q's had waited a minute or two to see what would happen, he switched them back on again just as suddenly. They did not catch him in the act, but were nevertheless well aware of what he was doing. The ghost always wore heavy boots, said Mr Q, and so his presence could be heard as he clumped up to the door and banged on it hard. Whenever Mr Q was near enough, he would rush to the door, but was never able to catch Archibald at it. Mr Q added that he had never been troubled by the ghost, neither did it throw things around or make itself a real nuisance, and so he had made no attempt to have Archibald exorcised. Mrs L, too, gradually learned to live with him, if she never actually came to love him.

On the A329, 15 miles south east of Oxford, **Wallingford** grew up in a strategic position where the ancient British Icknield Way crosses the Thames. The bridge at Wallingford is first recorded in 1141, the present one being of 13th-century workmanship rebuilt in 1751 and 1809.

The town is an example of Saxon town planning, as is shown in the grid pattern of its streets, and it grew to be one of the largest defended towns in Wessex, with permission to strike coins in its own mint. Wallingford received a charter in 1155, thirty two years before London was granted one.

The medieval town had 11 parish churches, of which only 3 survive, although others are commemorated in street names. The oldest church, St Leonard's, has Saxon herring-bone stonework and, although rebuilt, still has two Norman arches. The church fabric was badly damaged by Parliamentarian troops who were quartered there. St Lawrence's churchyard was transformed into an award-winning wildlife conservation area in 1996. The redundant St Peter's church, rebuilt in the 18th century, has a hollow spire which rises from an octagonal lantern to form a local landmark.

Wallingford Town Hall (1670) has the borough coat of arms. Its top storey houses a great chamber which has portraits of dignitaries by Lawrence and Gainsborough, a silver mace, and the town seal which dates back to the fifteenth century.

Although much of the medieval town has been destroyed by a series of fires, there are fine examples of buildings from later centuries, such as the Lamb Arcade, and the George Hotel which have been renewed and restored. The George, in Wallingford High Street, is a fine hotel offering all modern facilities, including its own website and resident ghost. Although its claims to be a 16th-century coaching inn, its origins may lie much further in the past, for it is the shadow of the once-mighty Wallingford Castle, and some claim that the George may have once been its dower house. The hotel was certainly once called the George and Dragon, and may have been a medieval hostelry. This was converted into the hotel which exists today by Geoffrey Baynton and his wife in 1517.

During the next century, Wallingford was a turbulent place in which to live, and, not surprisingly, fighting between soldiers and townspeople was only too common. In 1626, the landlord of the George was Francis Smith, a strong minded and independent man. One March evening, John Hobson, a Royalist came to the George to keep a tryst with Smith's daughter, an exceptionally lovely girl with long, black hair, to whom Hobson was engaged.

He had been there for only a few minutes, when a local troublemaker picked a quarrel with him. Hard words were exchanged, and soon the argument had turned into a full scale riot. Unfortunately, neither Francis nor his daughter were in the immediate vicinity to smooth things over, but were busy elsewhere in the hotel. By the time they hurried to the scene, Hobson was lying near to death in a pool of blood. There was no sign of the murderer. Hobson died in front of the horrified Smiths. His fiancee became hysterical with shock and grief, and was taken off to her own room while her beloved's body was prepared for burial Time and time again, the blood stains were scrubbed away from the floor of the death chamber, only to constantly reappear on the stone slabs.

After the funeral, life gradually returned to normal at the George for the rest of the population of Wallingford, but not for the bereaved girl upstairs in her room overlooking the High Street. Her mind had become unhinged, and she spent the rest of her life up there with her grief and her memories. As a form of therapy, she spent her days mixing soot from the fire with her own tears and painting teardrops all over the chamber walls.

Not very long afterwards, she too died, still whispering John Hobson's name.

Traces of the teardrops survived long enough for a journalist from the *North Berks Herald* to write in 1979 'and today we too can gaze at the very symbols traced so long ago by the young lady who was literally dying of love.'

Over the centuries there have been countless reports from guests occupying the Teardrop Room. In the 19th century, a guest, ignorant of the story, was woken by a thunder storm. In a flash of lightening, he was astounded to see a young girl busily drawing teardrops on the wall. Then the room went black again, and when the morning light came, she was gone. On the walls, though, there remained freshly made sooty teardrops, still damp. The most frequent comments made by those who have sensed something unusual about the Teardrop Room, mention a feeling of overwhelming sadness, and a mysterious figure which glides through the shadows there.

Holton Park Girls' Grammar School, now **Wheatley Park School**, is just outside Wheatley, on the A40, about 7 miles east of Oxford. Towards the end of the eighteenth century, Elisha Biscoe bought the Holton Estate, which at that time included a fine old castle surrounded by a deep moat. The date 1307 was to be seen inscribed on one of the corner stones which jutted out into the water. During the Commonwealth period, 1649-1660, Oliver Cromwell occupied the castle, then owned by the Whorwood family, and his daughter Bridget married the Parliamentary commander, Henry Ireton, in the chapel there.

Elisha Biscoe soon realised that the building was haunted, and promptly had it demolished, leaving not a single stone standing on another to give shelter to its ghostly residents. He then constructed the present house on the mainland; this house looks like a castle in miniature. Park

House was eventually converted into Holton Park Girls' Grammar School and a former pupil remembers vividly how her history teacher would tell the junior classes about the school ghosts. These confidences were not encouraged by the headmistress, and as a result, the descriptions were somewhat secretive and sketchy.

As far as the girls could gather, the ghostly company was supposed to consist of a nurse, with a small boy in her arms, running down the main staircase, known to them as the Front Stairs, together with a small dog which trots along a corridor upstairs, always managing to avoid being caught. Rumour had it that the nurse had tripped while going down the long stone staircase and had fallen onto the child, crushing him to death. Someone had suggested that the child might have been buried under the site of the Front Hall of the present building, although the grounds for such a supposition were never mentioned. The Front Hall is a large porch or foyer and is where the apparition is said to vanish.

No one at the school had heard of anyone having seen the ghosts, although few people were there after four in the afternoon; nevertheless, the girls were very keen on the idea of having their own resident ghosts. Perhaps it was just an old tale put about to frighten children, they reflected sadly, or maybe there really had once been ghosts, but they themselves had been scared off by the rock'n'roll which blared out on wet lunch breaks, or the patter of a hundred and fifty or so pairs of school footwear thundering up and down the haunted staircase?

More than twenty years later, the former pupil came across a book by Elisha Biscoe's great-nephew. Entitled, *Tyndale-Biscoe of Kashmir: An Autobiography*, it includes a description of Holton Park and the author's early days there. It also includes mention of the ghosts. From this, it was evident that what they had learnt at school was only the tip of the iceberg!

When he inherited Holton Park, Mr Tyndale-Biscoe soon found that the castle ghosts had migrated to the new building on the mainland. A succession of servants handed in their notice, and guests would complain of a sensation of there being strangers in the room when staying in a certain bedroom. This happened with an annoying regularity. When the writer was about twelve years old, he was standing at the bottom of the Front Stairs when he happened to look up and see a boy of his own age coming down the staircase as fast as he could go. When he put out his arm to restrain him, the strange boy veered sharply round the bottom of the stairs to avoid him and made for the Front Hall. Tyndale-Biscoe particularly noticed that the

Wheatley, Holton Park

other boy's feet did not touch the ground. When he reached the Front Hall, first the boy's head and then his body "went up suddenly in smoke, as if he had exploded." in a most unpleasant way.

Another apparition was seen by an aunt and uncle who were occupying the haunted bedroom. The lady became aware of it first and woke her husband who merely suggested that they should go straight back to sleep. She persisted, however, and eventually, when he was fully awake, he could see the white figure which stood near their bed. He called out, "Go away!" as he thought that it was one of the children playing a joke on them. As they watched, the white figure moved slowly across the room, and into a dressing room which they knew for certain was locked,

The next incident was the sighting, by a lawyer-cousin of the author Tom Tyndale, of a strange boy whom he at first took to be the footman. Then, the lady of the house noticed that the butler was looking very pale and drawn and told him to go and see the doctor. The butler replied that he was not at all unwell, but that he had seen a ghost in his own pantry. He went on to describe the 'very big woman' whom he had met there, dressed in a high-collared gown with puff sleeves, just as in the family's ancestral portraits. When asked if he had attempted to converse with her, the butler replied that he had been much too scared, and had fallen back against the wall out of her way. He assured Mrs Tyndale-Biscoe that, had he the talent, he could have painted the ghost lady from memory, so great an impact did she make on him.

Later Mrs Tyndale-Biscoe herself saw a small black dog trotting along the upstairs corridor; she tried to catch it without success. After this, some of the servants admitted that they too had seen the dog.

Some time after these sightings, the same aunt who had seen the white figure in the haunted bedroom, was in Switzerland when she got into conversation with another lady who showed great interest in hearing that the aunt's family had bought Holton Park. This lady asked if she had heard about the murder that had been committed there and, on learning that the aunt knew nothing about it, told her that the eldest son of a family living in the old house, had been murdered and secretly buried by his governess, and the assumption that the present house had been erected over the boy's grave could indeed be correct.

In his book, Mr Tyndale-Biscoe stresses that none of the children in his family was at all frightened by the ghosts, in fact quite the reverse for they wished that they would appear more often!

CHAPTER SIX:
THE VALE OF WHITE HORSE

Tourist Information Centres:
Abingdon: *25 Bridge Street, Abingdon, OX14 3HN*
Tel: 01235 522711
Faringdon: *7a Market Place, Faringdon, SN7 7HL*
Tel: 01367 242191
Wantage: *Vale and Downland Museum, 19 Church Street, Wantage,*
OX12 8BL   Tel: 01235 760176

The Vale of White Horse is arguably the most atmospheric of the districts of Oxfordshire. The most sparsely populated, too, it has dozens of listed prehistoric sites, together with the tiny spring-line villages which grew up centuries ago along the Ridgeway, one of the most ancient of British roadways. Although they lie within easy reach of motorway or railway, these little communities retain something of a flavour of Thomas Hardy's novels. At least three of the rivers have Ancient British names, the Charn, the Ock and the Stert, given by our Celtic ancestors centuries before their languages ever appeared in written form.

Despite all this history, accounts of unexplained happenings are disappointing, being sketchy and inconclusive in comparison with the rest of Oxfordshire. Very few apparitions have a factual basis, even less have a name, the notable exceptions being Robert and William, the monks at Charney Bassett.

Certain old favourites appear in the local newspapers to give atmosphere at Hallowe'en or Christmas, but there seems to be little substance in these stories. For example, at **Cumnor**, ghostly legions are said to tramp all night across the Hurst; **East Hanney** is haunted by a Grey Lady, and **Rowstock** is the scene of a reinacted coach crash.

A phantom horseman who was reported by three stable lads riding on the Downs near **Chilton**, brought back childhood memories to Mrs Betty Murray of Ardington, as she told the Oxford Mail in July 1979. Her mother, who used to cycle on the Downs, saw an identical sight one morning in 1920. The lone rider galloped into a patch of mist and never reappeared.

On 18th June 1983, the *Oxford Mail* covered the rumour then sweeping the Metal Box Company based on the former **Grove** airfield, near Wantage. The airfield was constructed in 1943, and used as a training base until 1944; it was taken over by the American Air Force two years later. This concerned late-night sightings of what appeared to be a phantom pilot, clad in flying gear and oxygen mask. In addition, excited workers spoke of a presence making itself felt in the area to the rear of the works. Plans of the site were brought out of storage, and these indicate that the ghostly flyer appeared near where the chapel of the airfield and officers' mess were situated during the War. It was suggested that he was a pilot who crashed his plane on landing and died as it went up in flames.

In the mid-Sixties, two sisters were driving through the village of **West Hendred** when they were involved in an accident with a ghost. The driver, Mrs Margaret Prior, told the *Oxford Times* (3rd January 1965) 'I couldn't possibly have avoided hitting him. I braked instantly as I thought I was going to kill him. I prepared myself for the bump, but nothing happened. I was shocked. My sister and I turned round but could see nothing or nobody. Since then we have heard an old man was killed in a car accident three years ago near the very spot.'

On 2nd January 1959, the *Didcot Advertiser* carried a description of a crowd of Cromwellian ghosts at **Ginge**. 'A barn seemed full of helmeted Puritans to the lady of the farm, one darkish night. The funny thing was they all seemed to be minus ankles and feet. In Cromwellian days, the floor of that barn had been nearly a foot lower!'

Situated some 7 miles south of Oxford on the A34, **Abingdon** was once the county town of Berkshire, but came over the border into Oxfordshire in 1974. It is the oldest continuously inhabited town in England, fending off claims from places like Colchester, whose evidence is documentary rather than archaeological. Abingdon is known for its river, its numerous sets of almshouses, three of which are in the grounds of St Helen's church, and for the remains of its abbey once one of the richest and most powerful in the country.

Abingdon guards its local traditions jealously. On the nearest Saturday to 19th June, the Mayor of Ock Street is elected by residents amid celebrations and Morris dancing; the Mayor holds office for the day. This custom is supposed to have originated in 1700, after a dispute between the residents of the street and other Abingdonians.

At times of national importance, like royal weddings, or the end of hostilities, a special type of bun is thrown to the crowds below from the Shire Hall. This custom dates from 1887, and specimens of buns are kept in the museum in the Hall.

Sad to relate, the ghosts of Abingdon are far from impressive.

The premises of the Abbey Press printing works in Stert Street now lie empty and silent. As far as anyone knows, that is, although just because the Press no longer occupies the building, it doesn't necessarily mean that there is no other activity going on inside. When workers at the Press were on the night shift there, a strange presence was sensed alongside the machinery, doors would bang, footsteps heard, and odd reflections and shadows noticed, usually between 2 and 3 o'clock in the morning.

Mr Joe de Souza had worked at the Press for more than two years before he became aware that there was anything strange about the premises. He recalled, 'It was last December. I heard a connecting door bang, which made me jump and then, as I was sitting at my machine, a reflection suddenly moved across the machine. I froze, but the reflection continued to move, so I am sure it was not coming from me. Then I felt this definite presence behind me. I didn't know about the ghost then, but I was certain someone was standing there. I looked round but didn't see anything. It was really frightening and I left work in a hurry.' Joe then found out that several of his work mates had had similar experiences. Joe then brought in his dog, which flatly refused to enter a certain room. After this, he never worked alone in the building again.

Another employee explained how he had been terrified by a shadow which had fallen across his work, and which passed behind the window beside him. This could not have been due to anything outside the building as this window was away from the street, facing the interior of the building. Abbey Press workers were unable to agree on the cause of the haunting, or indeed on its very existence. Some claimed that it was mere imagination on the part of their colleagues.

Early one evening a lady was making her way from the Vineyard and along the Motte, towards her home. She was laden up with shopping and, as she heard a man's heavy footsteps coming along behind her, she toyed with the idea of asking him if he would be kind enough to carry something for her. When the footsteps drew level with her, she turned to see a young clergyman and thought that he of all people was likely to assist. As they both stepped into the light of a street lamp, however, she noticed that the man's face was pale and drawn, as if he was both ill and unhappy. This made her change her mind, and while she was still looking at him uncertainly, the young clergyman faded away into thin air.

At Northcourt, on the outskirts of Abingdon, a phantom highwayman rides along to Bagley Wood by night. Proof that he is a real apparition is given by the fact that his horse takes him deep into the wood where, in former times, the path was on a much lower level.

On the River Ock, about eight miles west of Abingdon, **Charney Bassett** is small and very rural, its entire population numbering a few hundred souls; nevertheless, it is full of historical interest. St Peter's church is a small Norman structure, possibly on a Saxon site. The name of the village is made up of two elements: the first, Charn, the Celtic name for the River Ock, the second derives from the Norman Bassett family. A prehistoric earthwork in the parish, Cherbury Camp, is constructed like a hill fort despite its being built on flat ground.

In the Middle Ages, Charney Manor belonged to Abingdon Abbey and housed its abbot from the thirteenth to the fifteenth centuries. Today, it is still very attractive, with fine medieval features like the stone-arched windows and the solid oak beams in the ceilings. The Manor now belongs to the Society of Friends, and is used as a Quaker Meeting House and residential conference centre, although its use is by no means restricted to Society members.

Apart from the phantom Benedictine monks who have frequently been spotted in the Manor grounds and near the church, the chief resident ghosts are two monks. One is called Robert, the other William, and this is known because they have confided this information to recent visitors to the Manor. William has been noted on numerous occasions, usually in the former chapel which leads off the solar. He communicated to a lady visitor that he had something of interest to show her, and that he wished her to open a sixteenth-century Bible which is kept in the old chapel. When she did so, her hand was guided to the name 'William' which appeared in it, although in what context remains unknown. William is never reported to have spoken, but Robert seems more than willing to do so. The story goes, presumably spread by Robert himself, that he was a monk from Glastonbury Abbey who was sent to Charney to do penance for some unspecified misdemeanour. However, Robert seems to have died before he was able to accomplish this.

A reliable account was given in October 1976 by a lady from Harlow, in Essex, whose name does not appear to have been recorded. When she came to Charney, she had no idea of Robert's existence, past or present. She was sitting in the conference room, which was formerly the abbot's solar, when she was approached by a shadowy form which turned out to be Robert. He was wearing a brown habit, with the cowl pulled down low over his face. He made himself comfortable and then confided who and what he was, and why he had come to Charney Manor in the first place. It would be interesting to learn how Robert manages to communicate, presumably by thought processes rather than by actual words, as few people are likely to understand much spoken Middle English, Latin, or Old French. However, he achieved this, Robert told the lady and she duly passed on the information. When the Warden at the Manor, Mr John Reed, first heard about the visitor's experience, he was quite understandably rather sceptical. The lady informed Mr Reed that this was exactly the same experience undergone by several people whom Robert had decided to take into his confidence. The Warden had never encountered Robert and began to feel a tiny bit slighted. He did notice, though, that all the accounts tallied in every detail. Curiosity aside, Mr Reed said that he would welcome the chance to ask Robert for 400 years back rent which he had worked out must be owing. Perhaps this was the reason why Robert never manifested himself when Mr Reed was around.

The monk gradually established a routine of appearing on a regular basis, every six months or so, possibly unable to settle until his penance was out of the way. Eventually, people began to feel quite sorry for him.

The following year, however, the lady from Harlow wrote to the Manor cook about Robert and told her of something rather odd which had taken place there. She had been attending a prayer meeting, when she caught sight of a brown-robed figure which came into the meeting hall with the other people attending. Robert, for she felt certain that it was he, knelt down and, like everyone else, remained in silent prayer for about twenty minutes, after which he left.

Mr Reed said, on hearing her news, that he would note whether or not there were any further reports of Robert's appearing at Charney and, if there were none, he would assume that Robert had managed to get away, and had at last been accepted into heaven!

Faringdon's commanding site off the A420, 18 miles south west of Oxford, overlooks the ancient Ridgeway and the Thames Valley, and attracted Saxon settlers. It became a royal manor, where Edward the Elder died in 924. The Norman church of All Saints, standing on a little hill just off the Market Place, is said to be haunted by an unidentified member of the local gentry, the Pye family. Faringdon was besieged by Parliament during the Civil War

Henry Pye, a Poet Laureate, who, according to his contemporaries, produced the most atrocious poetry, built Faringdon House, in the Market Place, in 1780. He is referred to in satirical lines which became the nursery rhyme *Sing a Song of Sixpence*, being the 'pie' in question. The present house replaces one which was held for the King by the Royalist Sir Robert Pye, and bombarded by his Parliamentarian son, who strangely enough never succeeded in inflicting much damage.

On 23rd January 1964, the *Wantage Herald* described how the Wheeler family of Oriel Cottages was being pestered by poltergeist activity. This consisted of banging, rumbling and howling noises coming from the walls, furniture and even the family car. This had started shortly before the previous Christmas and became bad enough for the help of Canon CF Harman, an expert in psychic science, to be summoned. to the house. The Wheeler's had been advised to seek professional help by a Swindon medium who had identified the troublesome spirit as that of a former lodger who had committed suicide seventeen years previously. Mr Wheeler said, 'We think he is trying to get revenge because we only let him stop with us a week. He was a trouble maker. The same night he left our house, he lay down in front of a train outside Uffington Station and killed himself. The medium says he has contacted the same man; his name and description match. Now we are going to try with the help of the Canon to get rid of him.'

As is usual with poltergeist activity, children and young people were occupying the house at the time. The Wheeler family included Rosalie (5); Joy (10); Betty (15) and Colin aged nineteen. Canon Harman commented, 'This type of phenomenon is very common and a great deal of research has been done on the subject. Even though it may take a little time, I think we may be able to cure the trouble.'

In 1984, Mary D, a woman living alone - as she originally believed - in a fully modernised stone terraced house in **New Hinksey**, became convinced that she was sharing her home with a ghostly married couple. So certain did she become, that she invited M, a friend from work, to inspect the cottage, knowing that she was interested in such matters. This friend took Mary's story seriously for she was a down-to-earth Durham lass, heavily into feminism and the betterment of the working classes - the last person to entertain airy-fairy notions about the supernatural. This elderly couple occupied each side of the cottage's chimney breast, and their presence was felt strongly enough for Mary to be sure of their identity, even though she had never seen anything to verify this. Curiously, it was only when she entered the room unexpectedly that she sensed they were already in it.

Her friend arrived at the house, in a street off Oxford's Abingdon Road, about seven on a fine summer evening, and was shown the 'haunted' fireplace. This, in fact, contained no form of heating device, the whole house being centrally heated. They discussed just about everything and everybody except the old couple. Then, about 9.30, Mary dimmed the lights to demonstrate how the room appeared when the former residents were installed there. Mary sat herself down by the non-existent fire in what she sensed was the old man's favourite place. It should be mentioned that she had a very pronounced Durham accent, of which she was proud, but, as she chattered away, M became less and less conscious of it as Mary described how the original fireplace might have appeared.

As she went on talking about it, instead of saying 'I imagine. . .' or 'perhaps', Mary became quite definite as to what was where. She also started to use the present tense, 'Big fire, high up behind the bars. Comes right out here.' her hands indicating a large, square area.

'Is there a mantelpiece?' M asked, going along with what she supposed to be role-play.

'Yes, yes.' then, 'Cold, cold down this arm. Want to get to the fire. Want to light my pipe!' At this last comment, M sat up and took more notice; the voice was now clearly masculine, the accent had changed from Co Durham to Berkshire.

Mary went on, 'And boots, working boots, hurt my feet they do. Tired, very tired, and stiff. She rubbed her knees and thighs at this point.' 'Not like the pit men'. By this time M was feeling distinctly uneasy, although she still suspected that, in some inexplicable way, her hostess might be pulling her leg. It seemed unlikely, though, as by this time Mary was taking no notice of her whatsoever. The latter stood up, positioned herself in front of M, and demanded, 'What about that cup of tea you were talking about, then?' Tea had not been mentioned at any time during the evening. M stayed quiet, and at first there was no response, then, 'Cold, very cold down this side.' (arm raised, pointing), and then she realised that Mary was right, it was indeed very cold in the room. She put back on the Arran cardigan, which she had removed earlier because of the warmth.

'Let's put the lights on again, Mary, ok?' Still no reply, even when she was addressed directly by name. Enough was enough. M began to get worried. Wherever was that light switch? And how could she walk out and leave Mary, possessed as it were, sitting there murmuring into the semi-darkness in a voice which didn't belong to her? In desperation, M leant forward, calling, 'Mary, Mary!' and shaking her arm. Even then, she half-expected Mary to burst out laughing.

To her great relief, Mary jumped, twitched and shook her head two or three times. Slowly, she stood up and at last put the lights on. She looked pale and bewildered, as if she had just woken from a deep sleep. On being questioned, she appeared blank but indignant, as if suspecting that a trick had been played on her. Finally, she admitted that the last thing she remembered was attempting to explain how the cottage might once have looked.

126

No recollection of cold, of pipes, or boots, or of pitmen and stiffness. Would M swear to her that this was what she had spent the last hour or so talking about? And in a strange man's voice?

When the lights came back on again both women felt as if the room had been reclaimed. From that time onwards, Mary insisted that her house was a shared property; she was permitted the use of it in the hours of daylight, but as soon as dusk fell it reverted to `Them'.

A few weeks after the incident, Mary put the cottage up for sale.

Positioned on the Thames on the B4016, 1.5 miles south of Abingdon, **Sutton Courtenay** is a showplace which even the nearby cooling towers of Didcot Power Station cannot manage to spoil. A path leads down from the village to a bridge and weir on the river, and its winding main street is filled with trees and gardens, and ancient timbered and brick houses.

All Saints church dates from the 12th century and has in its churchyard the graves of the Earl of Oxford and Asquith, Prime Minister from 1908 to 1916. They built the house called The Wharf. Other occupants of the churchyard are the writer Eric Blair, better known as George Orwell, and Mrs Martha Pye who died in 1822 at the age of 117.

There was a royal residence at Sutton Courtenay which was visited by William the Conqueror, and in which Henry I's first child was born. It stood between the river and the village green, and parts of it have been incorporated into the medieval manor house.

Norman Hall dates back to 1190 and was extended in 1650, and again in 1905. The building's haunting consists of a very pleasant smell of flowers out of season. It is not apparent to all and sundry, notably only childless people, or those with adult offspring, in fact the opposite of a poltergeist. In addition, it is only noticeable in the oldest part of the Hall.

In 1964, the then owner, Mrs Doreen Bradshaw, told the *North Berks Herald*, 'It is a beautiful and most suitable ghost. Although I have never been aware of it, I am sure it is absolutely true. People who have stayed here, including a cousin and a friend, have said that they noticed it although I had not previously mentioned it to them.' Pleasant smells include those of narcissi in January, jasmine in April, and a strong spicy smell like cakes baking in the early morning before anyone in the house was up and about.

Lady Taylor of The Wharf, said, 'No one knows the origin of the ghost, but it has been handed down from owner to owner.' Unfortunately, by then older people who might have been able to throw some light onto the mystery had either left the village or died. The previous owner of the Hall told Mrs Bradshaw that once, when she was writing a letter, the smell became so strong that she turned round, fully expecting to find someone standing behind her.

On another occasion, a painter and decorator working in the building asked where the flowers were that smelled so lovely. There were none in the house. Other people who have experienced the ghostly perfume of Norman Hall say it is more like incense than flowers.

The other haunting in Sutton Courtenay is far from pleasant. In 1824, Daniel Grimshaw was executed for infanticide, and was soon adopted as resident bogeyman by parents in the area. It is said that Grimshaw committed some unspeakable act when murdering his small daughter, and this gave rise to the story that he had turned into a vampire. He is reputed to walk at the aptly named Purgatory Farm, near where Didcot Power Station is today. He has also been seen at night in a field near Hobbyhorse Road, on Milton Trading Estate nearby, although it is possible that he has since been exorcised by twentieth-century commerce.

Wantage is a market town on the A338, 15 miles south west of Oxford. Some of the town's early inhabitants lived in a 5-room Roman villa, complete with a hypocaust, on what is now Chainhill Farm.

Wantage's most famous son is King Alfred, who was 'born at Wantage (849), died at Winchester' as the local saying goes. His statue has pride of place in the market place. It is a smaller version of the one at Winchester, sculpted by Count Gleichen, and given to the townspeople in 1877. Saxon Wantage was burnt down by Danish raiders, an unusual event in this part of the country, and modern Wantage dates mainly from the 17th and 18th centuries.

Wantage formerly had two churches occupying the same churchyard, one being destroyed in the 19th century. The survivor, St Peter and St Paul, is medieval, and probably succeeds a Saxon minster church. It contains a large brass to Sir Ivo Fitzwarren (died 1412) who is thought to be the father of Alice, who married Dick Whittington. Another member of the Fitzwarren family, Sir William, lies in the church with his wife, also named Alice.

Across from the church is the Vale and Downland Museum, housed in a former doctor's surgery.

Ickleton Road, which runs along the ancient Roman route, is believed to be haunted by the figure of a man. He follows people silently, without any audible footsteps, and without altering his pace. The figure has been seen crouching on all fours like some sort of animal, and passing clean through a brick wall. On one occasion, when someone went to investigate, he found the figure running alongside him in a menacing way. Fearing an attack, he struck out first, only to find that his fist came up against - nothing! Then the figure just vanished.

April Fool's day was the chosen time for a haunting in Springfield Road. In April 1967, Mrs Ann Pettifer found her grandmother dead in bed there, and afterwards, claimed Mrs Pettifer, the old lady returned to haunt the house each 1st April. Manifestations included smoke in a room where there was no fire or similar traceable source; chairs thrown around the room first thing in the morning; and a bathroom heater which suddenly started to work again after a year of disuse; a smashed mirror, and wine bottles which moved unaided from a shelf to the larder floor. According to the *Oxford Mail*, 29th March 1979, Mrs Pettifer hoped that when the family moved to a new house elsewhere in Wantage, they would be free of the unwelcome incidents.

Miss Jessie Gibbs of Trinder Road had the same hope when she moved to Mill Street. Miss Gibbs had been forced to share her former home with a poltergeist which also smashed a mirror, and locked the bathroom door from the inside.

When she moved, Miss Gibbs naturally assumed that she would be able to leave her 'friend' behind in the Trinder Street house, but it had other ideas. She had been there about a year and lulled into a false sense of security by the lack of activity, when the poltergeist struck. Miss Gibbs was hosting a committee meeting when a table lamp went dim and the room suddenly became cold, despite a roaring open fire. Miss Gibbs put this down to the poltergeist standing in front of the fire. She informed the *Oxford Mail*, 3rd November 1967, that she was quite accustomed to poltergeist presence as she had experienced 'all sorts of visitations' during her childhood in a house in Newbury Street, where the Regent Cinema now stands.

'One shocking night,' for example, her pillow was tugged from under her head. Miss Gibbs saw her first ghost in about 1920 when a figure walked straight past her one night, and through a wall. Some years later she heard a 'sickening' footstep on the landing, which was also heard by her mother. Mrs Gibbs saw the shadow of a, 'grotesque' figure by the door of her bedroom.

When she was in Trinder Road, Jessie smelt what she thought was brown paper smouldering. This smell changed to that of 'spent' gunpowder after a time, and this was also smelt by Mrs Gibbs and some lodgers. Miss Gibbs believed that the burning was caused by an old warrior making a fire, as a battle was fought nearby. Her current 'friend', she added, was of nuisance value rather than really frightening.

By Letcombe Brook, on the outskirts of the town, lives 'the gentlest ghost', as the *Didcot Advertiser*, 2nd January 1959, calls the little old man who may be encountered there. Unfortunately, the newspaper gave no further details at the time, and none seem to have emerged since.

A more fearsome haunting dates back to at least July, 1914, when the farmer who owned the meadows nearby, would relate to his family how, in the grey light of dawn, he used to meet a strange warrior dressed in mail, as he collected his cows for milking. The farmer referred to the soldier as a friend, and would pass the time of day with him each time that they met.

One day in early August, the farmer appeared at breakfast seeming somewhat upset. He had met his old friend as usual, but, as soon as the warrior crossed the Letcombe Brook, the farmer heard the sound of dozens of horses splashing about in the water. Although there was no trace of any animals, he could clearly see the water being churned up by invisible hooves, causing foamy wavelets to reach the banks. The train of horses moved onwards, leaving the farmer to get his cows in for milking as usual.

The journalist comments that it would have been interesting to discover whether or not the phantom troops returned in 1939 to come to the aid of the country.

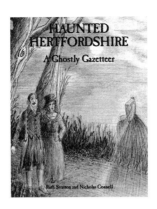

HAUNTED HERTFORDSHIRE
by
Nicholas Connell and Ruth Stratton

The most extensive collection of the county's ghosts ever written, with over 300 stories. Many are little-known and previously unpublished, having been hidden away in the vaults of Hertfordshire Archives and Local Studies. Others are up to the moment accounts of modem hauntings in the words of those who have experienced them. All supported by dozens of rare and evocative pictures, an outline of the latest theories and diary dates of regular apparition appearances.

Stories feature a feast of phantoms, including grey ladies, dashing cavaliers, spectral transport, headless horsemen and a gallery of Kings and Queens. Locations include Bishops Stortford, Datchworth, Harpenden, Hertford, Hitchin, Hoddeson, St. Albans, Ware and Watford.

The
Book
Castle

THE LAST PATROL
Policemen Killed on Duty while Serving in the Thames Valley
by Len Woodley

This book details those Policemen who have been killed on duty by a criminal act within the area now covered by the Thames valley Police - namely the counties of Berkshire, Buckinghamshire and Oxfordshire. It ranges from a Constable who, in the 1860s, died in Oxford just days after the formation of one of the constituent forces that made up the present-day Thames Valley Police and must surly be one of the shortest serving Policemen in this country, to the truly terrible day at Hungerford in the late 1980s, when so many people, including a traffic Constable, were murdered and others wounded in that picturesque Berkshire town. It encompasses Police officers encountering poachers, ejecting some drunken men from a public house, checking details of members of the visiting forces involved in a fracas in wartime England, attempting the apprehension of burglars and questioning some vicious, "stop at nothing" criminals over their behaviour in a motor car.

These police officers all started their day as normal, not one gave a thought to the possibility that he might be sent to a life-threatening job.

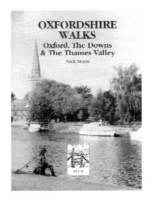

OXFORDSHIRE WALKS VOLUME 1
Oxford, The Cotswolds & The Cherwell Valley
&
OXFORDSHIRE WALKS VOLUME 2
Oxford, The Downs & The Thames Valley
by Nick Moon

Two titles each containing thirty circular walks. The two titles together provide a comprehensive coverage of walks throughout the whole of Oxfordshire (except the Chiltern part already covered in "Chiltern Walks: Oxfordshire and West Buckinghamshire" by the same author). The walks vary in length from 3.3 to 12.0 miles, but the majority are in, or have options in, the 5 to 7 miles range, popular for half- day walks, although suggestions of possible combinations of walks are given for those preferring a full day's walk.

Each walk gives details of nearby places of interest and is accompanied by a specially drawn map of the route, which also indicates local pubs and a skeleton road network.

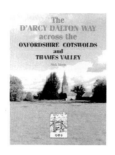
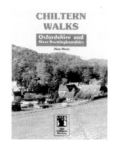

THE D'ARCY DALTON WAY
Across the Oxfordshire Cotswolds and Thames Valley
by Nick Moon

This guide to the D'Arcy Dalton Way replacing the original guide written and published by the late Rowland Pomfret on behalf of the Oxford Fieldpaths Society in 1987 and now out of print; describes both the route of the D'Arcy Dalton Way itself and eight circular walks using parts of its route ranging in length from 4.0 to 13.4 miles. The text of the guide to the way and each circular walk gives details of nearby places of interest and is accompanied by specially drawn maps of the route which also indicate local pubs and a skeleton road network. Oxfordshire County Council has kindly organised the acquisition and erection of special signposts for the D'Arcy Dalton Way.

CHILTERN WALKS
Oxfordshire and West Buckinghamshire by Nick Moon

This book is one of a series of three to provide a comprehensive coverage of walks throughout the whole of the Chiltern area (as defined by the Chiltern Society). The walks included vary in length from 3.0 to 10.9 miles, but are mainly in the 57 mile range popular for half-day walks, although suggestions of possible combinations of walks are given for those preferring a full day's walk. Each walk gives details of nearby places of interest and is accompanied by a specially drawn map of the route which also indicates local pubs and a skeleton road network.

Books Published by THE BOOK CASTLE

COUNTRYSIDE CYCLING IN BEDFORDSHIRE, BUCKINGHAMSHIRE AND HERTFORDSHIRE: Mick Payne. Twenty rides on and off-road for all the family.

PUB WALKS FROM COUNTRY STATIONS: Bedfordshire and Hertfordshire: Clive Higgs. Fourteen circular country rambles, each starting and finishing at a railway station and incorporating a pub stop at a mid way point.

PUB WALKS FROM COUNTRY STATIONS: Buckinghamshire and Oxfordshire: Clive Higgs. Circular rambles incorporating pub-stops.

LOCAL WALKS: South Bedfordshire and North Chilterns: Vaughan Basham. Twenty-seven thematic circular walks.

LOCAL WALKS: North and Mid Bedfordshire: Vaughan Basham. Twenty-five thematic circular walks.

FAMILY WALKS: Chilterns South: Nick Moon. Thirty 3 to 5 mile circular walks.

FAMILY WALKS: Chilterns North: Nick Moon. Thirty shorter circular walks.

CHILTERN WALKS: Hertfordshire, Bedfordshire and North Bucks: Nick Moon.

CHILTERN WALKS: Buckinghamshire: Nick Moon.

CHILTERN WALKS: Oxfordshire and West Buckinghamshire: Nick Moon. A trilogy of circular walks, in association with the Chiltern Society. Each volume contains 30 circular walks.

OXFORDSHIRE WALKS: Oxford, the Cotswolds and the Cherwell Valley: Nick Moon.

OXFORDSHIRE WALKS: Oxford, the Downs and the Thames Valley: Nick Moon. Two volumes that complement Chiltern Walks: Oxfordshire, and complete coverage of the county, in association with the Oxford Fieldpaths Society. Thirty circular walks in each.

UNEXPLAINED OXFORD & OXFORDSHIRE: Marilyn Yurdan. The unexplained in all its guises in one of the country's most historic towns and the villages of the rest of the county.

THE D'ARCY DALTON WAY: Nick Moon. Long-distance footpath across the Oxfordshire Cotswolds and Thames Valley, with various circular walk suggestions.

THE CHILTERN WAY: Nick Moon. A guide to the new 133 mile circular Long-Distance Path through Bedfordshire, Buckinghamshire, Hertfordshire and Oxfordshire, as planned by the Chiltern Society.

CHANGES IN OUR LANDSCAPE: Aspects of Bedfordshire, Buckinghamshire and the Chilterns 1947-1992: Eric Meadows. Over 350 photographs from the author's collection spanning nearly 50 years.

JOURNEYS INTO BEDFORDSHIRE: Anthony Mackay. Foreword by The Marquess of Tavistock, Woburn Abbey. A lavish book of over 150 evocative ink drawings.

COCKNEY KID & COUNTRYMEN: Ted Enever. The Second World War remembered by the children of Woburn Sands and Aspley Guise. A six year old boy is evacuated from London's East End to start life in a Buckinghamshire village.

CHANGING FACES, CHANGING PLACES: Post war Bletchley and Woburn Sands 1945-1970: Ted Enever. Evocative memoirs of post-war life on the Beds/Bucks borders, up to the coming of Milton Keynes new town.

BUCKINGHAM AT WAR: Pip Brimson. Stories of courage, humour and pathos as Buckingham people adapt to war.

WINGS OVER WING: The Story of a World War II Bomber Training Unit: Mike Warth. The activities of RAF Wing in Buckinghamshire.

JOURNEYS INTO BUCKINGHAMSHIRE: Anthony Mackay. Superb line drawings plus background text: large format landscape gift book.

BUCKINGHAMSHIRE MURDERS: Len Woodley. Nearly two centuries of nasty crimes.

WINGRAVE: A Rothschild Village in the Vale: Margaret and Ken Morley. Thoroughly researched and copiously illustrated survey of the last 200 years in this lovely village between Aylesbury and Leighton Buzzard.

HISTORIC FIGURES IN THE BUCKINGHAMSHIRE LANDSCAPE: John Houghton. Major personalities and events that have shaped the county's past, including Bletchley Park.

TWICE UPON A TIME: John Houghton. North Bucks short stories loosely based on fact.

SANCTITY AND SCANDAL IN BEDS AND BUCKS: John Houghton. A miscellany of unholy people and events.

MANORS and MAYHEM, PAUPERS and PARSONS: Tales from Four Shires: Beds., Bucks., Herts. and Northants: John Houghton. Little known historical snippets and stories.

THE LAST PATROL: Policemen killed on duty while serving the Thames Valley: Len Woodley.

FOLK: Characters and Events in the History of Bedfordshire and Northamptonshire: Vivienne Evans. Anthology of people of yesteryear -arranged alphabetically by village or town.

JOHN BUNYAN: His Life and Times: Vivienne Evans. Highly praised and readable account.

THE RAILWAY AGE IN BEDFORDSHIRE: Fred Cockman. Classic, illustrated account of early railway history.

A LASTING IMPRESSION: Michael Dundrow. A boyhood evacuee recalls his years in the Chiltern village of Totternhoe near Dunstable.

ELEPHANTS I'LL NEVER FORGET: A Keeper's Life at Whipsnade and London Zoo: John Weatherhead. Experiences, dramatic and sad, from a lifetime with these well-loved giants.

WHIPSNADE MY AFRICA: Lucy Pendar. The inside story of sixty years of this world-renowned institution. Full of history, anecdotes, stories of animals and people.

GLEANINGS REVISITED: Nostalgic Thoughts of a Bedfordshire Farmer's Boy: E.W. O'Dell. His own sketches and early photographs adorn this lively account of rural Bedfordshire in days gone by.

BEDFORDSHIRE'S YESTERYEARS: The Rural Scene: Brenda Fraser-Newstead. Vivid first-hand accounts of country life two or three generations ago.

BEDFORDSHIRE'S YESTERYEARS: Craftsmen and Tradespeople: Brenda Fraser-Newstead. Fascinating recollections over several generations practising many vanishing crafts and trades.

BEDFORDSHIRE'S YESTERYEARS: War Times and Civil Matters: Brenda Fraser-Newstead. Two World Wars, plus transport, law and order, etc.

DUNNO'S ORIGINALS: A facsimile of the rare pre-Victorian history of Dunstable and surrounding villages. New preface and glossary by John Buckledee, Editor of The Dunstable Gazette.

DUNSTABLE DOWN THE AGES: Joan Schneider and Vivienne Evans. Succinct overview of the town's prehistory and history - suitable for all ages.

HISTORIC INNS OF DUNSTABLE: Vivienne Evans. Illustrated booklet, especially featuring ten pubs in the town centre.

EXPLORING HISTORY ALL AROUND: Vivienne Evans. Planned as seven circular car tours, plus background to places of interest en-route in Bedfordshire and parts of Bucks and Herts.

PROUD HERITAGE: A Brief History of Dunstable, 1000-2000AD: Vivienne Evans. Century by century account of the town's rich tradition and key events, many of national significance.

DUNSTABLE WITH THE PRIORY: 1100-1550: Vivienne Evans. Dramatic growth of Henry I's important new town around a major crossroads.

DUNSTABLE IN TRANSITION: 1550-1700: Vivienne Evans. Wealth of original material as the town evolves without the Priory.

DUNSTABLE DECADE: THE EIGHTIES: A Collection of Photographs: Pat Lovering. A souvenir book of nearly 300 pictures of people and events in the 1980's.

STREETS AHEAD: An Illustrated Guide to the Origins of Dunstable's Street Names: Richard Walden. Fascinating text and captions to hundreds of photographs, past and present, throughout the town.

DUNSTABLE IN DETAIL: Nigel Benson. A hundred of the town's buildings and features, plus town trail map.

DUNSTAPLELOGIA: Charles Lamborn. Facsimile of a well-respected mid-Victorian town history, with a number of engravings og local buildings.

DUNSTAPLE: A Tale of The Watling Highway: A.W. Mooring. Dramatic novelisation of Dunstable's legend of Dunne the Robber - reprinted after a century out of print.

25 YEARS OF DUNSTABLE: Bruce Turvey. Reissue of this photographic treasure-trove of the town up to the Queen's Silver Jubilee, 1952-77.

DUNSTABLE SCHOOL: 1888-1971. F.M. Bancroft. Short history of one of the town's most influential institutions.

BOURNE and BRED: A Dunstable Boyhood Between the Wars: Colin Bourne. An elegantly written, well illustrated book capturing the spirit of the town over fifty years ago.

OLD HOUGHTON: Pat Lovering. Pictorial record capturing the changing appearances of Houghton Regis over the past 100 years.

ROYAL HOUGHTON: Pat Lovering. Illustrated history of Houghton Regis from the earliest of times to the present.

WERE YOU BEING SERVED?: Remembering 50 Luton Shops of Yesteryear: Bob Norman. Well-illustrated review of the much loved, specialist outlets of a generation or two ago.

A BRAND NEW BRIGHT TOMORROW... A Hatters Promotion Diary: Caroline Dunn. A fans account of Luton Town Football Club during the 2001-2002 season.

GIRLS IN BLUE: Christine Turner. The activities of the famous Luton Girls Choir properly documented over its 41 year period from 1936 to 1977.

THE STOPSLEY BOOK: James Dyer. Definitive, detailed account of this historic area of Luton. 150 rare photographs.

THE STOPSLEY PICTURE BOOK: James Dyer. New material and photographs make an ideal companion to The Stopsley Book.

COMPLETELY HATTERS: An A-Z of Luton Town: Dean Hayes. Major stars and incidents throughout the good days and not so good in the club's history.

PUBS and PINTS: The Story of Luton's Public Houses and Breweries: Stuart Smith. The background to beer in the town, plus hundreds of photographs, old and new.

LUTON AT WAR - VOLUME ONE: As compiled by the Luton News in 1947, a well illustrated thematic account.

LUTON AT WAR - VOLUME TWO: Second part of the book compiled by The Luton News.

THE CHANGING FACE OF LUTON: An Illustrated History: Stephen Bunker, Robin Holgate and Marian Nichols. Luton's development from earliest times to the present busy industrial town. Illustrated in colour and mono.

WHERE THEY BURNT THE TOWN HALL DOWN: Luton, The First World War and the Peace Day Riots, July 1919: Dave Craddock. Detailed analysis of a notorious incident.

THE MEN WHO WORE STRAW HELMETS: Policing Luton, 1840-1974: Tom Madigan. Fine chronicled history, many rare photographs; author~served in Luton Police for fifty years.

BETWEEN THE HILLS: The Story of Lilley, a Chiltern Village: Roy Pinnock. A priceless piece of our heritage - the rural beauty remains but the customs and way of life described here have largely disappeared.

KENILWORTH SUNSET: A Luton Town Supporter's Journal: Tim Kingston. Frank and funny account of football's ups and downs.

A HATTER GOES MAD!: Kristina Howells. Luton Town footballers, officials and supporters talk to a female fan.

LEGACIES: Tales and Legends of Luton and the North Chilterns: Vic Lea. Mysteries and stories based on fact, including Luton Town Football Club. Many photographs.

THREADS OF TIME: Shela Porter. The life of a remarkable mother and businesswoman, spanning the entire century and based in Hitchin and (mainly) Bedford.

HARLINGTON - HEYDAYS & HIGHLIGHTS: Edna L. Wisher. One of Bedfordshire's most historic villages, Harlington's yesteryears are seen through the eyes of one of its most empathetic residents.

FLITWICK: A DAILY TONIC: Keith Virgin. Written as a "Book of Days" containing extracts from the Flitwick Parish Magazine and local newspapers of around 100 years ago.

FARM OF MY CHILDHOOD, 1925-1947: Mary Roberts. An almost vanished lifestyle on a remote farm near Flitwick.

STICKS AND STONES: The Life and Times of a Journeyman Printer in Hertford, Dunstable, Cheltenham and Wolverton: Harry Edwards.

CRIME IN HERTFORDSHIRE Volume 1 Law and Disorder: Simon Walker. Authoritative, detailed survey of the changing legal process over many centuries.

THE LILLEY PICTURE BOOK: Betty Shaw. A picture book depicting village activities during the late nineteenth century and mainly the twentieth century.

JOURNEYS INTO HERTFORDSHIRE: Anthony Mackay. A foreword by The Marquis of Salisbury, Hatfield House. Introducing nearly 200 superbly detailed line drawings.

HAUNTED HERTFORDSHIRE: Nicholas Connell. Ghosts and other mysterious occurrences throughout the county's market towns and countryside.

LEAFING THROUGH LITERATURE: Writers' Lives in Herts and Beds: David Carroll. Illustrated short biographies of many famous authors and their connections with these counties.

A PILGRIMAGE IN HERTFORDSHIRE: H.M. Alderman. Classic, between-the-wars tour round the county, embellished with line drawings.

THE VALE OF THE NIGHTINGALE: Molly Andrews. Several generations of a family, lived against a Harpenden backdrop.

SUGAR MICE AND STICKLEBACKS: Childhood Memories of a Hertfordshire Lad: Harry Edwards. Vivid evocation of gentle pre-war in an archetypal village, Hertingfordbury.

SWANS IN MY KITCHEN: Lis Dorer. Story of a Swan Sanctuary near Hemel Hempstead.

MYSTERIOUS RUINS: The Story of Sopwell, St. Albans: Donald Pelletier. Still one of the town's most atmospheric sites. Sopwell's history is full of fluctuations and interest, mainly as a nunnery associated with St. Albans Abbey.

THE HILL OF THE MARTYR: An Architectural History of St.Albans Abbey: Eileen Roberts. Scholarly and readable chronological narrative history of Hertfordshire and Bedfordshire's famous cathedral. Fully illustrated with photographs and plans.

THE TALL HITCHIN INSPECTOR'S CASEBOOK: A Victorian Crime Novel Based on Fact: Edgar Newman. Worthies of the time encounter more archetypal villains.

HARE & HOUNDS: The Aldenham Harriers: Eric Edwards. Detailed highly illustrated history of a countryside institution.

SPECIALLY FOR CHILDREN

VILLA BELOW THE KNOLLS: A Story of Roman Britain: Michael Dundrow. An exciting adventure for young John in Totternhoe and Dunstable two thousand years ago.

THE RAVENS: One Boy Against the Might of Rome: James Dyer. On the Barton Hills and in the south-east of England as the men of the great fort of Ravensburgh (near Hexton) confront the invaders.

TITLES ACQUIRED BY THE BOOK CASTLE

BEDFORDSHIRE WILDLIFE: B.S. Nau, C.R. Boon, J.P. Knowles for the Bedfordshire Natural History Society. Over 200 illustrations, maps, photographs and tables survey the plants and animals of this varied habitat.

BIRDS OF BEDFORDSHIRE: Paul Trodd and David Kramer. Environments, breeding maps and details of 267 species, with dozens of photographs, illustrations and diagrams.

A BEDFORDSHIRE QUIZ BOOK: Eric G. Meadows. Wide ranging quizzes and picture puzzles on the history, people, places and bygones of the county.

CURIOSITIES OF BEDFORDSHIRE: A County Guide to the Unusual: Pieter and Rita Boogaart. Quirky, well-illustrated survey of little-known features throughout the county.

THE BIRDS OF HERTFORDSHIRE: Tom Gladwin and Bryan Sage. Essays, maps and records for all 297 species, plus illustrations, photographs and other plates.

BUTTERFLIES OF HERTFORDSHIRE: Brian Sawford. History and ecological guide, with colour photographs and maps for nearly 50 species.

WELWYN RAILWAYS: Tom Gladwin, Peter Neville, Douglas White. A history of the Great Northern line from 1850 to 1986, as epitomised by the five mile stretch between Welwyn Garden City and Woolmer Green. Profusely illustrated in colour and black and white - landscape format.

LIFE AND TIMES OF THE GREAT EASTERN RAILWAY (1839-1922): Harry Paar and Adrian Gray. Personalities, accidents, traffic and tales, plus contemporary photographs and old o.s. maps of this charming railway that transformed East Anglia and Hertfordshire between 1839 and 1922.

THE QUACK: Edgar Newman. Imaginative faction featuring characters in a nineteenth-century painting of a busy Hitchin market scene - especially quack doctor William Mansell.

D-DAY TO ARNHEIM - with Hertfordshire's Gunners: Major Robert Kiln. Vivid, personal accounts of the D-Day preparations and drama, and the subsequent Normandy battles, plus photographs and detailed campaign maps.

THE BOOK CASTLE
12 Church Street, Dunstable
Bedfordshire LU5 4RU
Tel: (01582) 605670 Fax (01582) 662431
Email: bc@book-castle.co.uk
Website: www.book-castle.co.uk